W9-BSV-654

LINUS PAULING

Makers of Modern Science

LINUS PAULING
Scientist and Advocate

David E. Newton

☑ Facts On File®

AN INFOBASE HOLDINGS COMPANY

LINUS PAULING: Scientist and Advocate

Facts On File, Inc.
460 Park Avenue South
New York NY 10016

Library of Congress Cataloging-in-Publication Data
Newton, David E.
    Linus Pauling: scientist and advocate / David E. Newton.
        p. cm. — (Makers of modern science)
    Includes bibliographical references and index.
    ISBN 0-8160-2959-8
        1. Pauling, Linus, 1901—Juvenile literature. 2. Biochemists—
United States—Biography—Juvenile literature. 3. Chemists—United
States—Biography—Juvenile literature. [1. Pauling, Linus, 1901– .
2. Chemists.] I. Title. II. Series.
QP511.8.P37N48 1994
540' .92—dc20
[B]   93-31719

A British CIP catalogue record for this book is available from the British Library.

Facts On File books are available at special discounts when purchased in bulk quantities for businesses, associations, institutions or sales promotions. Please call our Special Sales Department in New York at 212/683-2244 or 800/322-8755.

Text design by Ron Monteleone
Layout by Robert Yaffe
Cover design by Catherine Rincon Hyman
Printed in the United States of America

RRD FOF 10 9 8 7 6 5 4 3 2 1

This book is printed on acid-free paper.

For Betsy, our Friend
Thanks for being there when we needed you.

CONTENTS

1

LINUS PAULING: TRAITOR OR HERO?

The early 1950s were an exciting time for biologists and chemists. For more than a decade, researchers had been debating one of the most fundamental questions in the life sciences: What is the nature of proteins?

Part of the answer to that question was already known. Scientists knew that, in the simplest possible sense, a protein is a long string of amino acids joined to each other by means of a group of atoms know as a peptide linkage. But what was the geometric arrangement of that long chain of amino acids? That question was critical since the biological function of a chemical molecule is determined to a large extent by the spatial configuration of that molecule.

The experimental evidence needed to answer that question already existed. That evidence consisted of a collection of X-ray diffraction patterns. X-ray diffraction patterns are produced when X rays are diffracted (bent) by the atoms in a molecule. Each specific arrangement of atoms produces a characteristic diffraction pattern.

The problem was that diffraction patterns are extraordinarily difficult to interpret. They consist of a few spots and arcs on a photographic plate. Figuring out what these spots and arcs tell about molecular structure was—and still is—a real challenge.

By 1951, researchers had proposed a variety of models for the protein molecule. One stood out among the rest. It was a model originally suggested by two American chemists, Linus Pauling and Robert Corey. In October 1950, Pauling and Corey had submitted a report to the *Journal of the American Chemical Society* in which they theorized that a protein molecule is arranged in a twisting, spiral-like shape known as an alpha helix.

Although the model was appealing in some ways, it proved unacceptable to a number of scientists. For one thing, Pauling and Corey argued that a single complete twist in the protein helix included 3.6 amino acids. Many of their colleagues found it hard to imagine that the "twist-number" was not a neat integral number such as 3 or 4.

By late 1951 a committee of the Royal Society of London, one of the world's most prestigious scientific societies, decided that a meeting on protein structure ought to be held to allow scientists to debate various protein models, including the Pauling- Corey model. They asked the eminent crystallographer, W. T. Astbury, to organize the meeting. Astbury, in turn, wrote Pauling to inquire if he or Corey and one of their colleagues could attend the meeting and defend their model. The meeting was scheduled to be held in London on April 28, 1952.

Pauling was eager to attend the meeting since most of the world's most important protein researchers planned to attend. It would be his first opportunity to argue face-to-face with those who questioned his model. Thus, on January 14, 1952, he submitted an application for a passport to attend the London meeting.

Normally, obtaining a passport in these circumstances would be a routine matter. Pauling was a United States citizen and never convicted of a crime. By law, he qualified to receive the passport.

However, the early 1950s were anything but normal times in the United States. The country was in the grip of McCarthyism, a political frenzy that raised doubt about the loyalty of millions of Americans. Pauling, who had frequently spoken out about the excesses of McCarthyism, had become suspect among government officials on both federal and state levels.

As a result, the U.S. Passport Office decided that it "would not be in the best interest of the United States" to issue Pauling a passport. It so notified him on February 14.

Pauling's response was to reapply immediately with a letter to President Harry S Truman on February 29, 1952. In his letter,

Pauling pointed out that he had been given the Presidential Medal for Merit for his services to the nation between 1940 and 1946. He went on to say:

> *I am now writing you, as President of the United States, to rectify this action, and to arrange for the issuance of a passport to me. I am a loyal and conscientious citizen of the United States. I have never been guilty of any unpatriotic or criminal act. I am confident that no harm whatever would be done to the Nation by my proposed travel. On the contrary, I feel sure that the announcement of the denial . . . would not be in the best interests of the United States.*

Pauling received his answer not from President Truman, but from presidential assistant William D. Hassett. Hassett wrote that the president had gone to Key West and that Pauling's letter would be referred to the State Department. Pauling followed up on this correspondence with a personal letter to Mrs. R. B. Shipley, chief of the Passport Office. In his letter, Pauling explained that the visit to England was for purely scientific purposes and a "brief vacation for my wife and me."

On April 18, Shipley wrote back to Pauling, saying that it would be "impossible to grant you a passport." By that time, however, Pauling was already in Washington, D.C., supposedly on his way to Europe. He went in person to the State Department to talk with Shipley and to ask her why the passport could not be issued. Shipley responded that the United States did not issue passports to known Communists, persons suspected of being Communist, or anyone who associated with Communists. At the last minute, Pauling had to change his plans and cancel his visit to England.

The consequences of the government's decision were profound. On a short-term basis, Pauling was, of course, unable to attend the London conference, thus preventing him from explaining and defending a model that was eventually widely accepted. But there may have been a more long-term effect also.

During 1951 and 1952, biologists and chemists in England were working diligently on a problem related to protein structure: the structure and function of nucleic acids such as DNA (deoxyribonucleic acid). By 1953, the American biologist James Watson and the English chemist Francis Crick were to solve this problem.

In one of the greatest accomplishments in recent scientific history, Crick and Watson found that the DNA molecule exists as an intertwined double helix.

Pauling had also been interested in nucleic acids and had been working on his own model since the late 1940s. Had he attended the London meeting, he might well have heard about the key bit of evidence that Watson and Crick eventually used to solve the DNA puzzle. That bit of evidence was an X-ray pattern obtained by Rosalind Franklin, working in the London laboratories of Maurice Wilkins. Franklin's photographs of DNA were the best currently available and, when properly interpreted, revealed the molecular architecture of DNA.

By accident, Watson saw Franklin's DNA photographs on January 30, 1953. Almost immediately, he knew that they held the information he and Crick needed to construct their DNA model.

Within less than two months, they had done so, an achievement for which they were awarded the 1962 Nobel Prize for physiology or medicine.

What if Pauling had also seen Franklin's photographs in late 1952? Would he also have known how to interpret them and how to construct a correct model of DNA? Of course, no one can answer that question. Given his success with model-building for protein and other complex molecules, the answer might very well be "yes." But given the United States government's rabid anti-Communist tone in 1952, there was never even a chance that Pauling would have had that opportunity.

The events surrounding the 1952 controversy reveal a great deal about the central character of this book, Linus Pauling. He was—and is—one of the greatest chemists of all time. His understanding of the chemical bond and of molecular architecture is probably unsurpassed in the history of chemistry.

But Pauling has always had a profound interest in a host of topics that go beyond scientific research. He was regarded as suspect by the U.S. government because of his earlier activities in programs of social reform. He need not have been a member of the Communist Party to have held progressive ideas that were vigorously opposed by the conservative philosophy of post–World War II America.

Nothing could be more symbolic of the man Linus Pauling than the fact that he is the only person ever to win two unshared Nobel Prizes, one for chemistry and one for peace. Even today, nearly a half century after his most enduring accomplishments in chemistry and peace, Pauling remains an active thinker, battler for causes, and source of controversy.

2

GROWING UP IN OREGON

The U.S. government's decision to deny Linus Pauling's passport application in 1952 illustrates the political fanaticism of the day. Whatever his political views, Pauling was widely recognized as one of the world's greatest living scientists. His monumental textbook, *The Nature of the Chemical Bond*, had been published 13 years earlier and was already recognized as a classic in its field. Within two years, he would be awarded the highest recognition a chemist can receive, the Nobel Prize.

Few residents of Oregon in the first decade of the century would have predicted, however, that this native son would rise to such heights a half century later. Pauling was born into a family of modest and sometimes difficult circumstances on February 28, 1901, in Portland, Oregon. Portland was the largest city in Oregon, but it was also a city that retained many characteristics of the Western frontier.

Linus's parents were Herman Henry William Pauling, a druggist, and Lucy Isabelle (Darling) Pauling, usually called Belle. Herman's parents were originally from Germany, by way of Missouri, while Belle's father was born in Beverton, Ontario, and her mother, in the Willamette Valley of Oregon. Two daughters soon joined the Pauling family, Pauline Darling on August 7, 1902, and Frances Lucille on January 1, 1904.

Business conditions were not good for Herman Pauling, and he moved four times in six years, trying to improve his family's living conditions. The first move, in 1903, took the family to Oswego, now a suburb of Portland, about seven miles south of the city. The Paulings lived in a one-room apartment while Herman scratched out a living as a druggist and a salesman. Pauling's biographer Florence Meiman White explains that "There was great unemployment in Oswego, so the only doctor left town. People came to Herman for free medical advice as well as for their medicines."

A year later, the Oswego experiment having failed, Herman Pauling moved his family again, this time to Salem. There he took a job as a traveling drug salesman for D. J. Fry, a druggist and jeweler. This move proved no more successful than did the one to Oswego, and in 1905, the Pauling family packed up again. This time their destination was Condon, a tiny town in the middle of northern Oregon, 40 miles south of the Washington border. Condon is still a remote outpost with a population of less than 1,000.

Herman Pauling chose this unlikely spot for his next home because Belle's parents had lived there for a number of years. There seemed to be a promise of emotional and perhaps financial support from the Darlings for the growing Pauling family. In any case, Herman opened a drugstore in Condon shortly after the family's arrival in April 1905.

Life in Condon for young Linus was probably much like what most young boys dream of: lots of free time, lots of outdoor life, and lots of sports. He spent much of his time with his best friend and cousin, Mervyn Stephenson, on the Stephensons' wheat ranch outside of town. And—not necessarily on any boy's list of most favored activities—he entered the Condon grammar school in 1906.

White writes that young Linus learned to shoot a gun from Mervyn's father, but he never actually killed an animal. "When the moment came to pull the trigger," she says, "he shut his eyes and turned his face away. He just could not shoot an animal."

Linus's short stay in Condon was to have an interesting and ironic footnote. The little Oregon town was eventually to produce not one, but two Nobel Prize winners. The second, in addition to Pauling, was W. P. Murphy, who won the 1934 Prize for physiology or medicine for developing a treatment for pernicious anemia, the disease that was to take the life of Linus's mother in 1926.

By 1909, it had become apparent that life in Condon was not all that the senior Pauling had hoped for either. Suitcases were packed, and once again, the Paulings were on the move, this time

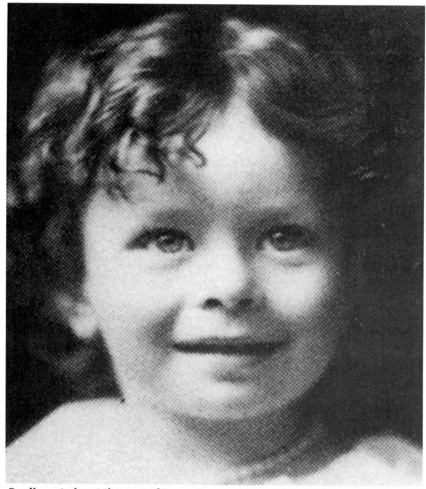

Pauling at about the age of two. (Courtesy of Mrs. Linda Kamb)

back to Portland, where Herman opened another drugstore. This move would be the last for Herman, however, as he died only a year later, on July 11, 1910, from a perforated stomach ulcer complicated by peritonitis.

Suddenly, Belle Pauling found herself a widow with a nine-year-old son and five- and eight-year-old daughters to support. This challenge would have been imposing in and of itself. But, by some accounts, Belle was not satisfied with a survival-level existence in any case. Pauling's biographer Anthony Serafini has suggested that Herman's death was hastened by "deepening melancholy over his wife's increasingly bizarre and unreasonable attitudes toward money and her obsession with finding ways for Linus to bring in extra income."

In the meanwhile, Linus was enrolled at Portland's Sunnyside Grammar School. Biographers look back on those early years for signs of Pauling's budding genius, but they are not especially successful. In fact, Pauling reports that it was not science, but mathematics, in which he first became interested. It was clear early on, however, that Pauling's intellect was one to be reckoned with. By the age of nine, he had read every book in the house, and his frustrated father had written to the local newspaper, the *Oregonian*, for advice.

"I am a father and have an only son who is aged 9 years, in the fifth grade, a great reader and is deeply interested in ancient history," Herman wrote. He then went on to say:

> In my desire to encourage and assist him in his prematurely developed inclinations, I ask some of the Oregonian's interested readers to advise me regarding the proper or at least the most comprehensive works to procure for him.

There is no evidence that Herman received any response to this letter.

Indications of a growing interest in science appeared soon enough, however. Pauling tells of making collections first of insects and then of minerals when he was 11 or 12 years old. Taking a very scientific approach, he not only collected objects but also read about them in library books and then proceeded to classify and catalog them.

The direction of Pauling's future scientific interests is reflected in his approach to the study of mineralogy. "I was not successful as a collector," he later recalled, "but I got a book from the library on mineralogy and I copied out tables of properties, hardness and various properties, onto sheets of paper and glued the papers to the wall in my workroom." In later years, it was primarily this kind of speculative, rather than experimental, research for which Pauling was to become famous.

The year 1914 was a turning point for Pauling in two ways. First, he graduated from the Sunnyside Grammar School and entered Portland's Washington High School. Second, and more important, he was introduced to the study of chemistry. The person responsible for the latter event was a friend named Lloyd Jeffress, who was to go on to become professor of psychology at the University of Texas.

Jeffress had set up a small laboratory in the corner of his bedroom where he carried out some simple experiments. After watching Jeffress conduct some experiments, Pauling became fascinated with chemistry. "I decided then to be a chemist," he has written, "and to study chemical engineering, which was, I thought, the profession that chemists followed."

Pauling's interest in chemistry was probably advanced somewhat by his teachers at Washington, William Greene and Pauline Geballe. But he also carried out a lot of research on his own in a small laboratory he built in his basement. He "borrowed" the chemicals he needed for his experiments from a small chemical laboratory at the abandoned Oregon Iron and Steel Company in Oswego. Since his grandfather was night watchman at a nearby plant, young Linus had access to the abandoned laboratory. With that guaranteed supply of materials, he said, "I became a chemist."

Pauling was also encouraged in his scientific interests by a retired mountain guide who befriended him and is remembered today only as "Mr. Yokum." Mr. Yokum was able to bring Linus some pieces of chemical equipment from the laboratory where he worked part-time. He also encouraged Linus to learn Greek since that was the language of "real scholars." By the time he was 13, Pauling had not only mastered some of that language, but was able to count to 100 in Chinese and to speak German, the language of his paternal grandparents.

Over the years, Pauling's passion for chemistry continued to grow. Writing in 1970 about his early years, he remembered that "I was simply entranced by chemical phenomena, by the reactions in which substances disappear and other substances, often with strikingly different properties, appear."

We have a glimpse of Linus Pauling the teenager from a diary that he kept during the last year of high school and the first year of college. At one point, for example, he lists a number of

"Tentative Resolutions" about how he will spend his time. The list includes items such as the following.

I will make better than 95 (Mervyn's record) in Analysis (Math).

(I made 99 6/11% in Analytic Geom) [added later]

I will take all the math possible.

I will make use of my slide rule.

I will make the acquaintance of Troy Bogart.

I must go out for track and succeed.

Linus was due to graduate from Washington High in 1917, but a problem developed. He had been under the impression that he could take two courses required for graduation, American History I and American History II, at the same time. By the time he found out that he had to take them in sequence, it was too late to schedule both courses.[*] As a result, he left high school in the spring of 1917 without a diploma. (This deficiency was remedied 45 years later when the high school awarded him his diploma. Even though he still lacked the necessary history credits, he had earned two Nobel Prizes in the interim.)

In the summer of 1917, Pauling faced a decision that many girls and boys have to make every year. Should he apply to go to college or start looking for work? His decision was a difficult one because his mother wanted him to stay at home and help with family finances. She still had two young children to raise, Pauline and Frances, and income from her boardinghouse was not enough to provide a comfortable life.

Belle encouraged Linus to learn his future career as an apprentice. "You can learn to be a chemical engineer while you're working," she said. "Your father became a druggist by working in a drugstore. Your grandfather became a lawyer by working in a lawyer's office," she argued.

---

[*] The situation described here is that given in White, p. 14. But Anthony Serafini, another of Pauling's biographers, quotes (p. 8) an article in the Portland *Oregonian* that claims that the course was a civics class, and that Pauling refused to take the class because he thought he could learn all he needed to know about civics by reading. In a 1964 interview, Pauling appears to confirm the White version of the story.

The decision was made all the more difficult because Linus was making good money working at a machine shop. He had earned $50 a month at first, then $75, and finally $100 a month. The owner promised him a raise to $150 a month if he would continue working at the shop instead of going to college . . . and $150 a month was a lot of money in 1917!

A section of Pauling's diary reveals his doubts about going on to Oregon Agricultural College (OAC).

Paul Harvey is going to O.A.C. to study chemistry—big, manly Paul Harvey, beside whom I pale into insignificance. Why should I enjoy the same benefits the [sic] he has, when I am so unprepared, so unused to the ways of man? I will not be able, on account of my youth and inexperience, to do justice to the courses and the teaching placed before me. But it is too late to change now, even if I wanted to, so I will only do my best. But perhaps every young college student feels as I do. I do not know. At any rate I will do my best.

Pauling as a student at Oregon Agricultural College, at far left. (Courtesy of Mrs. Linda Kamb)

But, in the end, Pauling's decision never seemed in doubt. He had developed a passion for learning and could not imagine *not* going on to college. So, to almost no one's surprise, he applied for and was accepted at the Oregon Agricultural College, now Oregon State University, in Corvallis. He left home for Corvallis in September, ready to begin a new phase of his life.

It didn't take long for Pauling to impress his teachers and fellow students. As Serafini has written, "He glided through the difficult first-year courses in engineering, chemistry, and math. His fellow students marveled and his intellect amazed the faculty."

But finances continued to be a problem. OAC charged no tuition, and fees and books were inexpensive. He lived cheaply in a boardinghouse, and then shared a room with a fellow student. But if his expenses were modest, so was his income. And since his mother could offer no support, Pauling had to earn enough himself to pay all his college expenses. He held all kinds of jobs, including working as a general handyman at a women's dormitory. He claims that he "worked a hundred hours a month and good hard work, too."

He describes a job delivering milk during his sophomore year, when he was 18 years old. It was, he remembers, "a very hard job, working eight hours every night from about eight o'clock to about four o'clock with a horse pulling the milk wagon and delivering milk to about 500 customers."

His diary records the budgeting he was obliged to do. He kept a detailed and precise record of where every penny went, from shoeshines to ice cream sundaes to books to a game of billiards. He made sure that his income and expenses balanced every day. When finances became especially tight, he cut back even further. At one point in his diary, for example, he notes, "Starting tomorrow, February 3, 1918, I am going to keep meals down to .50 per day."

His studies and work may have left little time for a social life. He is remembered by fellow students as having dated very little and having taken little part in campus life. In fact, Pauling was regularly subject to a practice know as "tubbing," a prank played on men who had no date on Saturday night. During "tubbing," the man was held under water by friends until he could force his way back up.

On one occasion, Pauling decided to get revenge for the tubbings. He apparently learned how to hold his breath for a long time by hyperventilating. When his friends put his head under water, he stayed under much longer than normal. They began to worry that he had drowned until he pulled out of the water and laughed at them.

As Pauling's freshman year came to a close, a new problem arose to divert his attention, World War I. The federal government had created a program called the Students Army Training Corps (SATC) to help qualified students stay in college. These students were expected to attend officer training school when they were not attending classes. After Pauling's stint with SATC in 1918, he got a job at a shipyard in Tillamook. He spent the rest of the summer of 1918 working at the shipyard with his cousin Mervyn Stephenson, of Condon, who was also a freshman at OAC.

Pauling's sophomore year mirrored and magnified his first year. Although he continued to do well in his classes, finances became more and more of a problem. His mother had become ill with pernicious anemia, and Linus now had to help support her and his sisters as well as himself.

Fortunately, Pauling was able to find a job as a paving-plant inspector for the State of Oregon during the summer of 1919. His job was to inspect new pavement and take samples back to the state laboratory for analysis. He earned $125 a month, all of which he sent back to his mother. He had almost no expenses since he lived in a tent with the workmen and ate with them in the mess. He expected that his mother would pay him back at the end of the summer and he would be able to return to Corvallis in the fall.

But his family's financial crisis only grew worse, and as fall approached, it became obvious that he could not go back for his junior year. Instead, he decided to keep his job as a paving-plant inspector and help his mother through the next year.

The year turned out quite differently, however. In November, Pauling received an offer from OAC to teach quantitative analysis in the chemistry department. That kind of offer would be almost unheard-of today. Pauling had only completed the course himself six months before. Now he was being asked to teach it!

Pauling during his senior year at OAC. (Courtesy of Pauling Archives; #324-1)

Nonetheless, Pauling accepted the offer. He returned to Corvallis and began his new $100-a-month teaching assignment. His schedule was apparently a demanding one. He supervised laboratories and gave lectures, spending a total of about 40 hours a week with students. That amounts to about four times the work of a regular college instructor today.

One positive aspect of his year as a teacher was the time he was able to devote to self-education. Even a 40-hour teaching schedule was less demanding than the busy two years of classes and work that had preceded them. Pauling chose to concentrate during 1919–20 on the works of two eminent chemists, Gilbert Newton Lewis and Irving Langmuir.

Until this time, Pauling had studied almost nothing about atomic physics. His introduction to Lewis and Langmuir, however, whetted his appetite for the subject. Before long, he developed "a strong desire to understand the physical and chemical properties of substances in relation to the structure of the atoms and molecules of which they are composed. This desire," he wrote in 1970, "has largely determined the course of my work for fifty years."

In the fall of 1920, Pauling was able to return to OAC as a student and begin his junior year. For whatever reason, he returned a somewhat changed person. He joined a fraternity, Delta Upsilon, and was elected to a well-respected military honor society, Scabbard and Blade. In addition, he took second place in an oratorical contest with a speech titled "Children of the Dawn."

Pauling's senior year at OAC was characterized by two great events, one a huge success story, the other an uncertain failure. The success story grew out of an offer made to Pauling in the fall of his senior year to teach a class in chemistry to home economics majors. One member of that class was Ava Helen Miller, the future Mrs. Pauling. Pauling reports that Miller answered one of his questions about ammonium hydroxide so well that "I thought I'd better keep an eye on her."

And indeed he did. Romance seemed to blossom almost immediately. In fact, the legend eventually developed that Ava Helen was the only woman Pauling ever dated at OAC. Although that story is almost certainly not true, it does illustrate the depth and strength of the bond that soon developed between them.

Today, a few letters between the young Linus and Ava Helen are preserved in the Pauling Archives at Oregon State University. The letters convey in a touching way the intense love that they eventually shared. In fact, the letters are so moving that a reader feels a sense of embarrassment at intruding on such a deep relationship.

Ava Helen Miller had been born on a farm near Oregon City on December 24, 1903. She grew up in a family that was neither especially poor nor rich, but in better circumstances that those of the Pauling family. She attended Salem High School before enrolling at OAC as a freshman in 1922.

The second event of significance in Pauling's senior year was his nomination for a Rhodes scholarship. In the first year that OAC was allowed to nominate Rhodes candidates, the faculty selected Pauling and Paul Emmett. Pauling certainly received high recommendations. One of his professors, Floyd Rowland, wrote that Pauling had "one of the best minds I have ever observed in a person of his age, and in many ways he is superior to his instructors."

Pauling did not receive a Rhodes scholarship, however. Observers then and now question how badly he really wanted a scholarship. One of his fraternity brothers reported that he spent the days before his Rhodes interview "reading some kind of story, a wild west magazine or mystery." Serafini lists a number of reasons that Pauling might not have wanted a Rhodes: his love affair with Ava Helen; his mother's illness; and his plans for graduate school. In any case, looking back from a vantage point of 60 years in the future, Pauling said that his failure to win a scholarship was "just good luck."

On June 5, 1922, Pauling received his bachelor of science degree from OAC. Three months later, he left for Pasadena and the California Institute of Technology where he began graduate work in physical chemistry. Another important and formative period of his life was about to begin.

CHAPTER 2 NOTES

p. 7   "There was great unemployment . . . " Florence Meiman White, *Linus Pauling: Scientist and Crusader* (New York: Walker and Company, 1980), p. 4.

p. 7   "When the moment came . . . " White, p. 5.

p. 9   "deepening melancholy . . . " Anthony Serafini, *Linus Pauling: A Man and His Science* (New York: Paragon House, 1989), p. 4.

p. 9   "I am a father . . . " Tom Hager, "Linus Pauling: His remarkable career," *The Oregon Stater*, February 1993, p. 10.

p. 9   "I was not successful . . . " Interview with Linus Pauling, John L. Heilbron, Office of the History of Science and Technology, University of California, March 27, 1964, Part One.

p. 10   "I decided then . . . " Linus Pauling, "Fifty Years of Progress in Structural Chemistry and Molecular Biology," *Daedalus*, Fall 1970, p. 988.

p. 10   "I became a chemist." Heilbron interview with Pauling.

p. 10   "I was simply entranced . . . " "Fifty Years of Progress," p. 989.

p. 11   "I will make better than 95 . . . " Pauling's diary, unpublished. Pauling Archives, Oregon State University, Corvallis.

p. 11   "You can learn . . . " White, p. 14.

p. 13   "He glided . . ." Serafini, p. 11.

p. 13   "a very hard job . . . " Heilbron interview with Pauling.

p. 16   "a strong desire . . . " "Fifty Years of Progress," p. 988.

p. 17   "one of the best minds . . . " As quoted in Serafini, p. 22.

3

THE CAL TECH YEARS

Like many college seniors, Linus Pauling was giving a lot of thought to graduate school during his last semester at OAC. There is little doubt that he could have been accepted almost anywhere in the nation. But he had focused his attention primarily on three institutions: the University of California at Berkeley, Harvard, and the California Institute of Technology (Cal Tech)* in Pasadena.

Berkeley ranked high on Pauling's list because G. N. Lewis was chair of its Department of Chemistry. Pauling was increasingly aware that the new view of chemical bonding offered by Lewis and Langmuir was likely to expand greatly chemists' understanding of molecular architecture. Working with Lewis would put Pauling in the forefront of the research that he had already chosen for his own career.

For whatever reason, however, Berkeley did not respond to Pauling's application in time. And Harvard removed itself from contention when its scholarship offer was inadequate for Pauling's financial needs. The best it could offer Pauling was a half-time instructorship that would have allowed him to finish his degree in five years.

In addition, Pauling's biographer Anthony Serafini hypothesizes that "the prospect of abandoning California for the bitter winters and crowded streets of Massachusetts Avenue was made all the more terrible by its proximity to the crowded and corruption-ridden city of Boston."

---

* Cal Tech is also known as C.I.T., an abbreviation that Pauling himself apparently prefers.

The choice fell, therefore, to Cal Tech. And so, in the fall of 1922, Pauling enrolled as a graduate student in physical chemistry at Pasadena. The decision was not an entirely satisfactory one. Ava Helen was still a sophomore at OAC, so she remained in Corvallis. The blossoming romance between the two made Pauling's move difficult, but he left for Pasadena nonetheless.

As it turned out, the choice of Cal Tech may have been just right, matching a brash, young, intellectually exciting institution with a graduate student who could be described in similar terms. Until 1920, the Pasadena institution had been known variously as Throop University, Throop Polytechnic Institute, and Throop College of Technology. Since its founding in 1891, it had had a relatively undistinguished academic reputation.

All of that had changed in about 1907, however, when George Ellery Hale, a member of the Throop Board of Trustees, suggested to his fellow trustees that they develop an outstanding institute for science and technology on their campus. Hale was director of the Mount Wilson Observatory at the time and one of the great entrepreneurs of science in the early part of this century.

Largely through Hale's efforts, a number of America's leading researchers began to relocate at Pasadena. Among these was perhaps the most famous physicist in America, Robert A. Millikan. Millikan left the University of Chicago in 1918 to become Cal Tech's first administrative head.

Another newcomer was the outstanding physical chemist, Arthur Amos Noyes. Noyes left the Massachusetts Institute of Technology in 1917 to establish the Gates Chemical Laboratory at Throop. He had a clear idea of the direction in which he wanted his chemistry department to go, and he chose faculty and students who would fit into that plan. Among those students was Linus Pauling.

The pursuit of Pauling by Noyes on behalf of Cal Tech is somewhat remarkable. OAC was not a particularly prestigious institution, and Pauling himself was not even a chemistry major. Historian John W. Servos has pointed out that OAC offered no graduate courses in physical chemistry and even its elementary course appeared to be "substandard." But Noyes obviously saw something in the young man from Oregon that showed promise, and he offered him a chance to prove himself in Pasadena.

Noyes was in contact with Pauling during the summer before he was to arrive in Pasadena. He sent Pauling the proofs of his new chemistry text, *Chemical Principles*, with instructions to solve all the problems in the first nine chapters of the book, more than 500 problems in all. Pauling completed the task before leaving for Pasadena, and later observed that it provided a better background in physical chemistry than had his OAC course in that subject. This incident provides support for the hypothesis made by one writer that "Perhaps Noyes saw in him [Pauling] the man he wanted to train as his successor" at Cal Tech.

Both Pauling and Noyes have commented on the extraordinary match between student and institution. At various times, Noyes referred to Pauling as "the exceptional fellow from Oregon," "his understudy," and "the most able chemist he had ever seen." In 1933, he remarked that "[w]ere all the rest of the Chemistry Dept. [at Cal Tech] wiped away except P., it would still be one of the most important departments of chemistry in the world."

In turn, Pauling has written that "[d]uring the last forty years I have visited universities all over the world. I now have the opinion that I had the greatest good luck in having gone to Pasadena in 1922. I do not think that I could have found better conditions for preparation for a career in physical chemistry anywhere else in the world."

In any case, Pauling's first glimpse of Cal Tech as he stepped off the train in the fall of 1922 may have been disarming. One writer has described the 30-acre campus as a collection of "dried, caked weeds, a run-down orange grove, and a handful of small sound oaks."

Still, the power of the institution was not its physical setting, but its faculty and student body. Twenty-nine graduate students were taught and supervised by 18 faculty members in three buildings. The small size of the college and its intellectual brilliance seemed to guarantee a productive learning atmosphere for almost any motivated student.

One of Pauling's colleagues, James Bonner, explains how the conditions at Cal Tech contributed to this atmosphere. He tells of twice weekly seminars that all teachers and students in the chemistry department were expected to attend. Each seminar "lasted from one to two hours and was a marvelous teaching device. The senior professors would decide on a topic, maybe statistical mechanics or whatever. You could go a lot deeper than in any course."

Pauling himself has described the intimate relationships that developed among students and faculty. He tells how Noyes took Pauling and other graduate students on camping trips to Palm Springs and invited them to be his guests at the Noyes oceanside home at Corona del Mar. Such occasions "gave opportunity for the unhurried discussions of scientific and practical problems" that were so important at the institution.

The first few months at Cal Tech must have been difficult ones for Pauling. Whatever he may have thought of his OAC education, it soon became obvious that his background was not as strong as that of his classmates. During a seminar in the spring of 1923, Professor Richard Tolman asked him a question that he couldn't answer. Pauling's response was, "I don't know; I haven't taken a course in that subject."

He was somewhat taken aback when a colleague stopped him after the seminar and told him, "Linus, you shouldn't have answered Professor Tolman the way you did; you are a graduate student now, and you are supposed to know everything." Little wonder that Pauling was later to confess that "there were so many gaps in my understanding that . . . often I did not know whether to attribute this failure to myself or to the existing state of development of science."

Soon after his arrival, Pauling was assigned to work with Roscoe Gilkey Dickinson on the topic of crystal structure. Dickinson had been recruited by Noyes also and had been awarded Cal Tech's first Ph.D. in 1920. Dickinson's specialty was X-ray crystallography, a method for determining the structure of minerals, crystals, and other substances.

X-ray crystallography had its origins in the work of the German physicist Max von Laue in the 1910s. The nature of X rays, discovered only a decade earlier, was still a matter of some dispute. Von Laue realized, however, that if they were waves, rather than particles, they would have wavelengths much shorter than the wavelengths of visible light. That fact, in turn, would suggest that X rays might be diffracted by the orderly arrangement of atoms in single crystals the way visible light is diffracted by evenly spaced lines on a diffraction grating.

In order to test this hypothesis, von Laue designed an experiment in which X rays were beamed at a crystal of copper sulfate. After a number of failures, he and his graduate students eventually produced a photograph consisting of smeared-out spots.

The photograph was of poor quality, but it confirmed von Laue's hypothesis. The pattern of spots in the diffraction photograph was caused by the arrangement of atoms in the copper sulfate. It was clear that, in principle, X-ray diffraction photography could be used to determine the structure of any substance composed of an orderly array of atoms or ions (that is, any substance that could be crystallized).

The techniques of X-ray crystallography were further refined by the father-and-son team of William Henry and William Lawrence Bragg. The Braggs developed mathematical formulas for calculating the wavelengths of X rays by crystal diffraction and improved methods for predicting crystal structure based on X-ray analyses. For their work in this field, the Braggs were awarded the 1915 Nobel Prize in physics. (Von Laue had won the same award a year earlier.)

Knowing of Pauling's interest in molecular structure, Noyes believed that Dickinson was the most appropriate advisor for his graduate work. It didn't take Pauling long to appreciate the complexities of diffraction analysis. He worked for two months with 15 different crystals, trying to find just the right one to analyze. Eventually he was "rescued by Dickinson," who brought him a specimen of molybdenite. After Dickinson prepared the specimen for Pauling, teacher and student worked together to determine its structure. The results of that work were published in 1923 as "The Crystal Structure of Molybdenite" in the *Journal of the American Chemical Society*. The paper was the first of more than 900 that Pauling was to produce in the next 70 years.

During his remaining years as a graduate student at Cal Tech, Pauling was to author six more papers including reports of the structures of magnesium stannide, hematite, corundum, and barite. His interests ranged far beyond the Gates Chemical Laboratory, however. Cal Tech expected its students to study a variety of sciences, a requirement to which Pauling had no objection. He also took courses in mathematics, physics, and astronomy, fields in which he was also exposed to some of the leading scholars of the day. He learned quantum mechanics, for example, from Arnold Sommerfeld and Paul Ehrenfest when each was a visiting professor at Cal Tech.

During his work on X-ray crystallography, Pauling developed a problem-solving approach that was to become his trademark years into the future. He describes this method as follows:

> *Really only a small fraction of the crystals that we attacked could be solved in terms of their structure by logical methods. My attitude was, why shouldn't I use the understanding that I have developed of the nature of crystals in inorganic substances and proceed to predict their structures? I would predict the structure and then I would calculate the X-ray pattern and if it agreed with the observed pattern, then I felt I had the right to say that it was the right structure.*

The irony of this story is that this method led, not only to some of Pauling's greatest accomplishments in determining the structures of molecules, but also, when adopted by Watson and Crick three decades later, to one of the most important single scientific discoveries of the 20th century, the structure of the DNA molecule.

In the spring of 1925, Pauling completed his requirements for a Ph.D. in chemistry with minors in mathematics and physics. He received that degree on June 12 with a *summa cum laude* distinction. His doctoral dissertation consisted of a series of papers resulting from his X-ray crystallography studies.

Two years before graduation, in the spring of 1923, one fact about Pauling's personal life was becoming more and more clear: His separation from Ava Helen was not working out. The couple decided to marry, even though she had not completed her studies at OAC. Thus, on June 17, 1923, the two were married in the home of Ava Helen's sisters in Salem, Oregon. The only honeymoon they could manage was the ride back to Pasadena in a Model T Ford.

Two years later, on March 10, 1925, the Paulings' first child, Linus Carl, Jr., was born in Pasadena. The Paulings eventually had three other children: Peter Jeffress, born on February 10, 1931; Linda Helen, born on May 31, 1932; and Edward Crellin, born on June 4, 1937.

The spring of 1925 was also a busy time as Pauling began to plan his postdoctoral studies. He applied for, and was eventually to receive, a National Research Council (NRC) fellowship. His expectation had been to work with Lewis at Berkeley, and Pauling had asked permission of him in 1924 to indicate those plans on his fellowship application. After Pauling had received the fellowship, however, Noyes convinced him to stay in Pasadena until he finished writing his X-ray crystallography reports.

The political intrigue that followed was an indication of Noyes's respect for Pauling and his eagerness to assure that Pauling would eventually return to Pasadena. First, Noyes agreed to allow Pauling to go to Berkeley, as his fellowship had specified. But then he also suggested that Pauling apply for a Guggenheim Fellowship, a more prestigious award.

Noyes further offered to pay for Pauling's boat ticket to Europe and to pay his expenses there until the Guggenheim was approved. "You know, it's so valuable to go to Europe," Noyes said, "you ought to go to Europe right away. I'm sure that you'll get the Guggenheim Fellowship; and the Institute will give you a $1000. And if you run out of money, I'll advance some money to you."

Noyes's motive was apparently his fear of losing Pauling to the University of California. In fact, the competition for Pauling's services seems to have been a real one. G. N. Lewis had actually visited Pasadena in 1925 to offer Pauling a position at Berkeley, an offer that Noyes never mentioned to Linus. "After some years," Pauling later said, "I realized Noyes was determined that I wouldn't set foot on the Berkeley campus. . . . Noyes was just determined that I should be a staff member here [at Cal Tech].

In any case, Pauling gave up his NRC fellowship and sailed for Europe in March 1926. There he spent two years studying with Arnold Sommerfeld, Niels Bohr, and Erwin Schrödinger, scientists who were reshaping humankind's understanding of physics, in general, and of the atom, in particular.

CHAPTER 3 NOTES

p. 19   "the prospect of abondoning . . . " Anthony Serafini,
           Linus Pauling: A Man and His Science (New York:
           Paragon House, 1989), p. 24.

p. 20   "substandard" John W. Servos, *Physical Chemistry from Ostwald to Pauling: The Making of a Science in America* (Princeton, NJ: Princeton University Press, 1990), p. 275.

p. 21   "Perhaps Noyes saw . . . " George W. Gray, "Pauling and Beadle," *Scientific American*, May 1949, p. 16.

p. 21   "the exceptional fellow . . . " As quoted in Servos, p. 296.

p. 21   "During the last . . . " Linus Pauling, "Fifty Years of Physical Chemistry in the California Institute of Technology," in *Annual Review of Physical Chemistry*, vol. 16, H. Eyring, ed. (Palo Alto, CA: Annual Reviews, Inc., 1965): p. 2.

p. 21   "dried, caked weeds . . . " Judith R. Goodstein, "Atoms, Molecules, and Linus Pauling," *Social Research*, Autumn 1984, p. 696.

p. 21   "lasted from one . . . " As quoted in Serafini, p. 28.

p. 22   "gave opportunity . . . " "Fifty Years of Physical Chemistry in the California Institute of Technology," p. 3.

p. 22   "I don't know . . . " Linus Pauling, "Fifty Years of Progress in Structural Chemistry and Molecular Biology," *Daedalus*, Fall 1970, p. 992.

p. 22   "rescued by Dickinson . . . " Linus Pauling, "Acceptance of the Roebling Medal of the Mineralogical Society of America," *The American Mineralogist*, March–April 1968, p. 527.

p. 24   "Really . . . " David Ridgway, "Interview with Linus Pauling," *Journal of Chemical Education*, August 1976, p. 473.

p. 25   "You know, it's so valuable . . . " Interview with Linus Pauling, John L. Heilbron, Office of the History of Science and Technology, University of California, March 27, 1964, Part One.

p. 25   "After some years . . . " Heilbron interview.

4

TWO YEARS IN EUROPE

For all his innate genius, Linus Pauling was also the beneficiary of having been born at the right time in history. The 1920s were a decade of profound revolution in the way scientists viewed matter and energy. It was Pauling's good fortune to be present as this revolution took place and to study with some of the great minds that brought the revolution about. But it was also his genius to be able to see how these changes were to bring about a corresponding revolution in chemical thought.

The revolution of the 1920s actually had had its beginnings in 1900 in the work of the German physicist Max Planck. Planck was able to solve an old and troubling problem involving the way heat is radiated by assuming that energy (at least in this case) occurs in the form of tiny packages that he called *quanta* (sing., *quantum*).

Planck's theory was startling because it suggested that energy might have characteristics that scientists had normally thought of as belonging to matter. The theory had to be taken seriously, however, for one important reason: It worked. Not only did it explain satisfactorily the previously unsolved problem of black-body radiation, but also it was soon applied (by Albert Einstein) in the solution of another theretofore peculiar phenomenon, the photoelectric effect.

The second key discovery leading to modern quantum theory was the discovery in 1923 by Prince Louis de Broglie of the wave nature of electrons (negatively charged subatomic particles). The French physicist was able to demonstrate that some properties of electrons can be understood only if one assumes that they are traveling through space in the form of waves, similar to light waves. Just as energy appeared to have matterlike properties, so, it seemed, could matter have energylike properties.

What followed, then, was an attempt by physicists to develop mathematical techniques that could be used to describe the dual properties of matter and energy, as expressed in quantum theory. One of those techniques was the wave equation, derived by the Austrian physicist Erwin Schrödinger in 1926. Schrödinger demonstrated that the position of the electrons in an atom could be accurately predicted if one assumed certain properties ("quantum numbers") for the electron and assumed that the electron moved in a wave that was described by his equation.

Pauling's course work at Cal Tech had been such that he could not have avoided hearing about the ideas of quantum theory. One of the faculty members with whom he studied and who had a strong influence on him was Richard Chace Tolman. From Tolman, Pauling learned relativity theory, statistical mechanics, and mathematical physics. In 1925, in fact, Pauling and Tolman had published a paper together using classical quantum mechanics to solve problems dealing with the heat properties of liquids cooled to absolute zero (-273.15°C or the temperature characterized by the complete absence of heat).

Pauling also heard about quantum theory from guest lecturers at Cal Tech. One of these, Arnold Sommerfeld, had developed the notion that electrons can travel around an atomic nucleus, not in perfect circles, but in elliptical orbits. This idea was to be incorporated into Schrödinger's wave equation as one of the electron's quantum numbers, its azimuthal quantum number. Quantum numbers are numbers that specify the characteristics of an electron in an atom. The first, or *principal*, quantum number (designated by the letter n) gives the average distance of the electron from the atom's nucleus. The second, or *azimuthal*, quantum number (designated by the letter l), describes the ellipticity of the electron's orbit. The third, or *magnetic*, quantum number (designated by the letter m) describes how an electron's orbital is orientated in space compared to other orbits. The fourth, or spin, quantum number (designated as s or m_s), tells the orientation of the electron's spin, clockwise or counterclockwise.

When the question arose in 1926 as to where Pauling was to spend his Guggenheim Fellowship, the choice was easy, the laboratories of the new pioneers in quantum theory. So, after a short vacation with Ava Helen in Italy, the two traveled on to Munich, where they arrived on April 20. For the next year, Pauling was to work with Sommerfeld at his Institute of Theoretical Physics.

Almost immediately, Pauling was confronted with the still-preliminary state of quantum mechanics. Sommerfeld had proposed a theory that assigned two quite different numerical values to a single property of the electron. He was certainly aware of this inconsistency, but he told his students to concentrate on the mathematical equations themselves, and not to worry about how they should be interpreted in terms of a physical model.

The fundamental question in Pauling's mind was how this new quantum mechanics could be applied to the topic in which he was

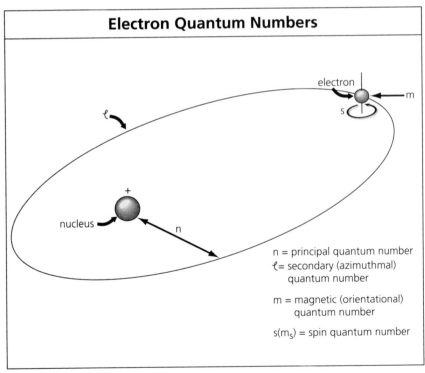

Electron Quantum Numbers

n = principal quantum number
ℓ = secondary (azimuthmal) quantum number

m = magnetic (orientational) quantum number

s(m_s) = spin quantum number

Figure 1

most interested, the structures of atoms and molecules. Was quantum mechanics "sufficiently close to being correct," he wondered, "so that if we solve the equation we'll get the right answers in relation to the properties of atoms and molecules?"

He was confident that the answer to this question was yes. He was already aware of the successful application by Heisenberg and Schrödinger of quantum mechanics to the understanding of simple atoms. What he hoped for now was "similar success . . . for more complex atoms, containing many electrons, and also for molecules and crystals."

By 1927, more evidence that quantum mechanics could be applied to chemical structure began to accumulate. The Danish physicist O. Burrau successfully used quantum mechanics to analyze the hydrogen molecule ion. He was able to predict values for the bond energy, bond length, and frequency of vibration for the ion that closely matched the values obtained experimentally for these properties.

There quickly followed two analyses of the hydrogen molecule based on Burrau's approach, one by E. U. Condon and the other by W. Heitler and F. London. There no longer seemed much doubt about the value of quantum mechanics in the analysis of atomic and molecular structure.

The successes of Burrau, Condon, Heitler, and London prompted Pauling to report some of his own quantum mechanical calculations on atomic and molecular properties. The paper he wrote, "The Theoretical Prediction of the Physical Properties of Many- Electron Atoms and Ions," was published in January 1927 in the *Proceedings of the Royal Society*. The paper ultimately became one of the most frequently cited of all his research papers. (The frequency with which a paper is cited by other scientists is often regarded as an indication of its importance and influence.)

During Pauling's stay in Munich, he received one piece of bad news. His mother, Belle, finally lost her long battle with pernicious anemia and died on July 12, 1926.

By the spring of 1927, Pauling had completed his work in Munich. The next stop on his European tour was Copenhagen, where he was to spend a month with Niels Bohr at the Institute for Theoretical Physics. While in Copenhagen, Pauling worked with the Dutch physicist Samuel Goudsmit, whose work on spectral lines eventually led to the discovery of the fourth, or spin, quantum number.

The European tour came to a conclusion with a five-month visit to the University of Zurich. There Pauling attended lectures by Schrödinger and Peter Debye. He also continued his quantum mechanical calculations on the interaction between two hydrogen atoms.

In some ways, Pauling's two years in Europe solidified the direction of his research for at least the coming decade. It was now clear that a technique derived from theoretical physics, quantum mechanics, could be applied to problems that are fundamentally chemical in nature—the way atoms bond with each other.

Historian John W. Servos has pointed out what a remarkable position Pauling was now in. As a result of his study in Europe, he had brought together two important, but formerly separate, traditions. On the one hand, he already knew a great deal about building models of atoms and molecules from his work on X-ray crystallography at Cal Tech. In his European studies, he had then learned a theoretical technique (quantum mechanics) for calculating the position of electrons in atoms and molecules. "Neither approach [by itself] as yet yielded much useful information about the nature of chemical bonds," Servos has written. "But together the two methods might be made to complement one another."

Pauling acknowledged the somewhat hybrid position in which he found himself. His research clearly did not fit into any traditional definition of chemical studies. "Some people seem to think that work such as mine, dealing with the properties of atoms and molecules, should be classed with physics," he wrote to Noyes in December of 1926, "but I, as I have said before, feel that the study of chemical substances remains chemistry even though it reach the state in which it requires the use of considerable mathematics."

By the summer of 1927, the Paulings were ready to return home. That statement could well have been more true for Ava Helen than for Linus. While her husband had been matching wits with some of the brightest, most exciting minds in the world, Ava Helen had little to do other than being a tourist. As Anthony Serafini has observed, she "was tiring of spending her days touring cathedrals and tending to the needs of her husband."

In addition, the Paulings missed their young son. They had decided in 1926 not to take Linus, Jr., to Europe with them, but to leave him with Ava Helen's parents. Mrs. Miller is reputed to have told her daughter and son-in-law that "You can't drag this infant halfway around the world. He'll be just fine here."

Still, it is not hard to understand how the long separation from their two-year-old son must have been very difficult for both parents. One can easily imagine why Ava Helen was "jumping with anticipation" as their departure time drew close.

As the ship sailed for America, a new position, assistant professor of theoretical chemistry, was awaiting Pauling at Cal Tech. Some of the accomplishments for which he was to become most famous and for which he was to win a Nobel Prize were also on the horizon.

CHAPTER 4 NOTES

p. 30   "sufficiently close . . . " Interview with Linus Pauling, John L. Heilbron, Office of the History of Science and Technology, University of California, March 27, 1964, Part Two.

p. 30   "similar success . . . " Linus Pauling, "Fifty Years of Progress in Structural Chemistry and Molecular Biology," *Daedalus*, Fall 1970, p. 993.

p. 31   "Neither approach . . . " John W. Servos, *Physical Chemistry from Ostwald to Pauling* (Princeton, NJ: Princeton University Press, 1990), p. 284.

p. 32   "was tiring . . . " Anthony Serafini, *Linus Pauling: A Man and His Science* (New York: Paragon House, 1989), p. 51.

p. 32   "You can't drag . . . " Florence Meiman White, *Linus Pauling: Scientist and Crusader* (New York: Walker and Company, 1980), p. 34.

p. 32   "jumping with anticipation . . . " Serafini, p. 51.

5

"THE NATURE OF THE CHEMICAL BOND"

Pauling returned to Pasadena in the fall of 1927, ready to assume his new job as assistant professor of theoretical chemistry. His return appears to have been tinged with some disappointment at not having received exactly the appointment he had expected. He told interviewer John Heilbron in 1964 that Noyes had offered him an appointment as "Assistant Professor of Theoretical Chemistry and Mathematical Physics." He was surprised to find upon his return, therefore, that the dual appointment had not worked out. For some reason, he was prevented from joining the physics department in addition to his chemistry appointment. Pauling wondered whether this decision reflected Millikan's preference to keep Linus out of the physics department.

This controversy reflects the ambiguous position in which Pauling found himself then, and has often found himself since. He has consistently referred to himself as a "chemist" or a "physical chemist." Yet it is clear that much of his early work was intimately involved with mathematics and physics. Indeed, his two years in Europe had provided him with contacts that many "real" physicists had not yet experienced.

The issue as to where Pauling "belonged" in the scientific community was not an entirely academic question. His broad background in mathematics, physics, and chemistry gave him a perspective on questions of atomic and molecular structure that someone trained more narrowly in chemistry might not have had.

In later years, his interest expanded even further into biology. Pauling's ability to interpret the phenomena of living organisms in terms of mathematical equations and atomic structure eventually made him one of the pioneers of the new science of molecular biology.

In any case, Pauling's first few years back at Cal Tech seemed to constitute a period of consolidation. He continued to do research on crystal structures and on the quantum mechanical analysis of atomic structure. His 30 publications between 1928 and 1931 dealt with topics such as "The Crystal Structure of Pseudobrookite," "The Crystal Structure of Topaz," "Quantum Mechanics of Nonpenetrating Orbits," and "Quantum Mechanics and the Chemical Bond."

Pauling lecturing at Cal Tech. (Courtesy of Pauling Archives; #324-47)

Included among these papers was one, "The Principles Determining the Structure of Complex Ionic Crystals," that outlined the rules now known as Pauling's Principles. These principles can be used to predict stable forms of crystalline substances. They are valuable in determining the diffraction patterns that can be expected from an X-ray analysis. Three of the six principles had been used earlier by, or at least were known to, other crystallographers, including William Lawrence Bragg. However, Pauling was the first to clearly state the complete set of principles.

During this period of consolidation, Pauling's reputation continued to grow by leaps and bounds. He was promoted to associate professor at Cal Tech in 1929 and then to full professor in 1931 (at the age of only 30). For a period of five years beginning in 1929, Pauling also traveled each spring to Berkeley, where he lectured at the University of California. He spent between one and two months at Berkeley each year, alternating his teaching between chemistry and physics.

Pauling's visits to Berkeley were especially valuable because they allowed him to spend time with G. N. Lewis. The two chemists spent a great deal of time talking about new ideas concerning the nature of chemical bonds, a topic on which Pauling was soon to write his most famous works. Pauling writes that the visits to Berkeley were a great pleasure and that he was "in retrospect, rather surprised that he and I did not write a paper together."

Pauling's first book was also published in 1930. He and the Dutch-American physicist Samuel A. Goudsmit coauthored *The Structure of Line Spectra*. The book contains large sections taken from Goudsmit's dissertation along with additional material that he sent to Pauling. Much of the final writing and translation were completed by Pauling, however.

The summer of 1930 found Pauling off to Europe once again. The trip began with a visit to Lawrence Bragg's laboratory at the University of Manchester. In principle, that visit might have been a very productive one, bringing together two of the greatest scientists of the day. In fact, it did not work out that way. Pauling said later that the visit was "a disappointment" to him. "I had essentially no contact with Bragg. And they failed to ask me to present a seminar talk, say, on my work, because I had done a great deal of work that bore on what Bragg's laboratory was doing." Bragg's unhappiness with Pauling's earlier failure to give him credit for the rules of crystal structure seems to have been a factor for this professional slight.

From Manchester, Pauling traveled on to Munich, where he visited again with Sommerfeld, and then on to Ludwigshafen, where he met Herman Mark. From Mark, Pauling learned about the use of electron diffraction techniques for the determination of molecular structure. Electron diffraction analysis is similar to X-ray diffraction except that it uses a beam of electrons rather than a beam of X rays and the target is in gaseous form rather than crystalline form.

After this return to Cal Tech, Pauling directed one of his students, L. O. Brockway, to construct an electron diffraction machine. By using the technique, Pauling and his students determined the molecular structure of more than 225 substances over the next 25 years.

The year 1931 marked an important turning point in Pauling's career. His years of thinking about and working with quantum mechanics as a tool for understanding molecular structure finally bore fruit. On April 6, his paper on the nature of the chemical bond was published in *Journal of the American Chemical Society (JACS)*. The 34-page paper was eventually followed by six more papers on the same topic over the next two years. In those papers, Pauling developed a single coherent theory that described the way atoms bond to each other—a theory that is still used in essentially the same form by chemists today.

The question of how atoms combine with each other goes back long before the modern atomic theory had even been proposed. The Roman philosopher Lucretius had suggested as early as the first century B.C. that the fundamental particles of matter contain fishhook-like appendages that allow them to combine with each other.

Two thousand years later, Linus Pauling was teaching a theory of atoms that differed very little from that of Lucretius. In 1919, chemists often described atoms as consisting of hooks and eyes through which they could be joined to each other. Pauling explains that he was "reasonably well satisfied with this explanation of chemical bonding."

During his tenure at OAC as instructor of quantitative analysis in 1919–20, however, Pauling was introduced to a new concept of the chemical bond, that of G. N. Lewis. Over the first two decades of the 20th century, Lewis had developed the fundamental concepts of the modern theory of chemical bonding. In 1902 he suggested that one way in which atoms can combine is through the loss and gain of electrons. For example, a sodium atom combines with a chlorine atom when it gives up the single electron in its outermost energy level to the chlorine atom. A chemical bond formed in this way is called an *ionic bond*.

By 1916, Lewis had proposed a second method by which bonding can occur. In some cases, he suggested, two atoms may share a pair of electrons between them. The attraction of the nuclei of both atoms for the same pair of electrons results in a *covalent bond* between the two. (This idea was put forward at about the same time by Irving Langmuir.)

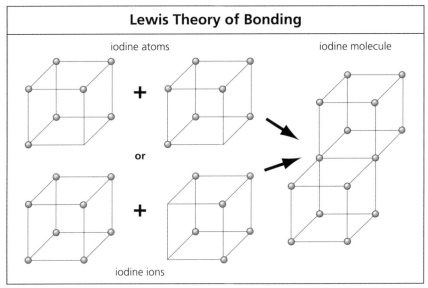

Figure 2

Pauling's contribution to the development of bond theory was to examine ionic and covalent bonding by applying the principles of quantum mechanics. Over a period of less than a decade, he transformed Lewis's somewhat simplistic theory of the chemical bond into a highly sophisticated analysis of the way electrons are shared between two atoms. In that process, Pauling eventually developed almost all of the most fundamental principles of the modern theory of chemical bonding, including hybridization, resonance, and electronegativity. Small wonder that some observers have called Pauling's 1939 book, *The Nature of the Chemical Bond, and the Structure of Molecules and Crystals*, one of the half dozen most important books in the history of chemistry. The book eventually went through three editions and was translated into French, Japanese, Russian, and Spanish.

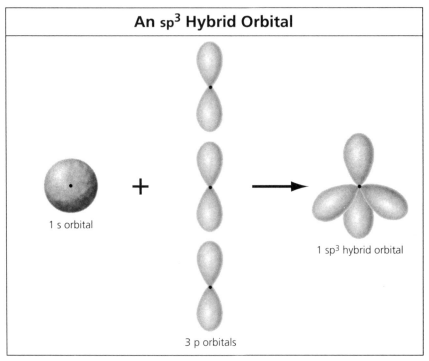

Figure 3

One of Pauling's first breakthroughs concerned the hybridization of electrons in the carbon atom. Earlier studies had shown quite conclusively that the four outermost electrons in the carbon atom occupy different energy levels, known as the 2s and 2p orbitals. Thus, one would expect carbon to form at least two different kinds of bonds. Yet, when carbon bonds to other atoms, the four bonds it forms are identical with each other.

Pauling explained this apparent discrepancy by assuming that the four bonding electrons in carbon undergo some kind of hybridization during bonding in which all assume a new configuration that makes them equivalent to each other. He referred to this new configuration as an sp^3 orbital.

In a second line of research, Pauling examined in greater detail the contrast between ionic and covalent bonding. As late as 1930, it was still not clear which type of bond occurred within the well-studied hydrogen chloride (HCl) molecule. Pauling applied quantum mechanics to the question and found that some intermediary structure between a pure ionic and pure covalent bond resulted in the most stable configuration for the HCl molecule.

He concluded, therefore, that bonding did not necessarily involve an all-or-nothing, ionic-or-covalent bond choice. In fact, most bonds fell somewhere along a continuum between these two extremes.

To quantify this discovery, he proposed a concept known as electronegativity. An element's electronegativity is a measure of its relative ability to attract the two electrons in a covalent bond. When an element with a high electronegativity combines with one having a low electronegativity, the former is able to capture both electrons, and an ionic bond results. When two elements with roughly equal electronegativities react, each exerts a roughly equal pull on the electrons, they share the electrons equally, and a covalent bond results.

The puzzle of the structure of the benzene molecule also yielded to Pauling. Benzene had long posed a problem for chemists because its molecular formula (C_6H_6) appears to be grossly inconsistent with the chemical properties expected of a molecule with this structure. In 1865, the German chemist Friedrich Kekulé had suggested an answer to this problem. He hypothesized that a benzene molecule consists of six carbon atoms arranged in a ring, with alternate single and double bonds between adjacent atoms. In order to account for benzene's chemical properties, he further proposed that the molecule could assume two distinct forms in which the position of the double bonds continuously shifted back and forth in the molecule.

For more than 60 years, chemists accepted the Kekulé model even though it was not entirely successful. Around 1930, Pauling asked what new information quantum mechanics would provide about benzene. He found that the most stable form of the benzene molecule was neither one nor the other of the Kekulé structures, but some intermediary form. "With quantum mechanics," he later said, "the actual structure involved can be described as a super-position of the two Kekulé structures. So described, the interconversion would be so rapid that there would be no hope of describing molecules with just one structure."

The "rapid interconversion" between two structures was given the name *resonance*. Pauling had been able to demonstrate that the state of a molecule can be determined more correctly by using quantum mechanics than by using predictions based on classical atomic theory. This breakthrough was soon put to use in the determination of other molecular structures.

Pauling's ideas about resonance, electronegativity, orbital hybridization, and other phenomena were laid out in his seven articles in the *Journal of the American Chemical Society* and eventually formed the core of his 1939 book, *The Nature of the Chemical Bond*. Interviewers have asked Pauling why it took so long for the book to appear. His answers suggest that, while he knew a great deal about bonding during the early 1930s, his ideas were still developing and maturing. By the mid-1930s, he was ready to begin recording those ideas in more permanent form. "By 1935," he has written, "I felt that I had an essentially complete understanding of the nature of the chemical bond. This understanding had been developed in large part through the direct application of quantum mechanical principles to the problem of the electronic structure of molecules."

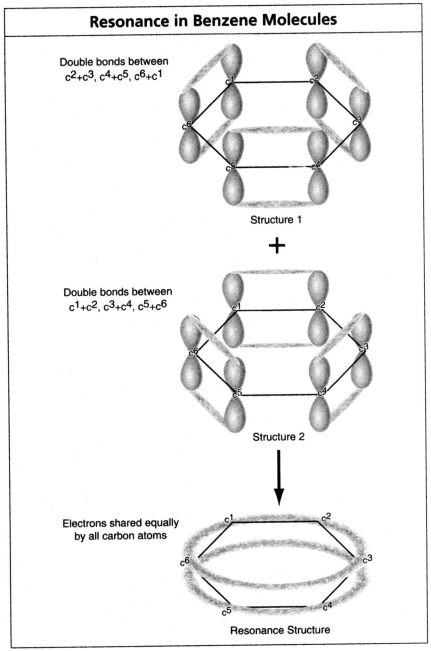

Resonance in Benzene Molecules

Double bonds between
$c^2 + c^3$, $c^4 + c^5$, $c^6 + c^1$

Structure 1

+

Double bonds between
$c^1 + c^2$, $c^3 + c^4$, $c^5 + c^6$

Structure 2

Electrons shared equally
by all carbon atoms

Resonance Structure

Figure 4

As the seven *JACS* papers emerged, so did Pauling's reputation among his colleagues. In September of 1931, he was the first recipient of the American Chemical Society's A. C. Langmuir Prize in Pure Chemistry for "the most noteworthy work in pure science done by a man under 30 years of age." He was also being courted by other institutions who felt that his presence on their faculty would enhance their own prestige. Among these were Harvard and the Massachusetts Institute of Technology (M.I.T.). Physicist John Slater at M.I.T. wrote Pauling in 1931 offering him a salary of $8,000 (a lot of money in those days), a full professorship, and a joint appointment in physics and chemistry.

For a variety of reasons, Pauling did not accept the M.I.T. or Harvard offer. According to biographer Serafini, weather was almost certainly a factor since both Linus and Ava Helen preferred the "warmth and familiarity of Pasadena" to the "awful snow in Cambridge." Pauling himself has said that "I just thought I wouldn't feel at home there . . . I just didn't want to live in Cambridge." He did agree, however, to spend a term at M.I.T. during the spring of 1932.

The M.I.T. visit was apparently not a very successful one, either professionally or personally. Serafini points out that "the stay [at M.I.T.] was not the most productive period of Pauling's career," and he alludes to the "family squabbling" that took place during the months in Cambridge. Life was undoubtedly made more difficult for Ava Helen since she had one-year-old Peter to care for in addition to Linus, Jr., and was pregnant with Linda, born at the end of their East Coast stay.

As 1933 drew to a close, Pauling could look back with satisfaction on a half decade of enormous accomplishment. Awards such as an honorary doctorate from his alma mater, now Oregon State University, and election to the National Academy of Sciences were recognition of the achievements he had already recorded. A majority of scientists—including some of the most brilliant—have begun to slacken off at this point in their lives, willing to rest on their laurels. Such was not to be the case with Pauling, however. In fact, he was about to set out on an entirely new line of research that was to yield yet more revelations about the structure of matter.

CHAPTER 5 NOTES

p. 35   "in retrospect . . . " Linus Pauling, "Pauling on G. N. Lewis," *Chemtech*, June 1983, p. 334.

p. 35   "I had essentially . . . " Horace Freeland Judson, *The Eighth Day of Creation* (New York: Simon & Schuster, 1979), p. 77.

p. 37   "reasonably well satisfied . . . " Linus Pauling, "Fifty Years of Progress in Structural Chemistry and Molecular Biology," *Daedalus*, Fall 1970, p. 990.

p. 40   "With quantum mechanics . . . " David Ridgway, "Interview with Linus Pauling," *Journal of Chemical Education*, August 1976, p. 474.

p. 40   "By 1935 . . . " "Fifty Years of Progress," p. 998.

p. 42   "warmth and familiarity . . . " Anthony Serafini, *Linus Pauling: A Man and His Science* (New York: Paragon House, 1989), pp. 61, 75.

p. 42   "I just thought . . . " Interview with Linus Pauling, John L. Heilbron, Office of the History of Science and Technology, University of California, March 27, 1964, Part Two.

p. 42   "the stay . . . " Serafini, p. 61.

6
THE TURN TO BIOCHEMISTRY

Until the 1930s, the study of living systems had not been of much interest to Linus Pauling. As he confessed in a 1978 interview, he had "never had a course in biology. No course in biochemistry either." In fact, he had remarked in a 1924 letter to a friend that the graduate work in biochemistry at Cal Tech was "interesting but I wouldn't want to do it." Such comments are especially intriguing in view of the fact that Pauling was soon to turn his attention to the study of molecules that are of importance in biological phenomena. So successful was this line of research to be that Pauling is now regarded as one of the founders of the modern science of molecular biology, which, he claims, "one might call modern biology."

Pauling's conversion to biological topics resulted from two forces. The first was the changing character of Cal Tech. When Pauling arrived in Pasadena, Cal Tech was strongly oriented toward the physical sciences, with almost no courses available in the life or social sciences or in the humanities. That situation began to change in 1929, however, when the famous geneticist Thomas Hunt Morgan was persuaded to leave Columbia University to establish a new biological department at Cal Tech. Morgan's department soon included some of the greatest names in modern genetics, Theodosius Dobzhansky, Calvin Bridges, and Alfred Sturdevant among them.

Genetics was the one field of biology in which Pauling might be expected to develop an interest. It was far more precise and quantitative than most other biological fields. Pauling writes that, by 1931, he "had become interested enough in genetics to present a seminar describing a theory of the cross-over of chromosomes that I had developed."

Soon, a mutual sense of respect began to develop between Pauling and the geneticists. The latter recognized in Pauling a person who respected their field and to whom they could go for help. As one of the group later explained, "he could understand what you were telling him that you wanted done, and he could tell you what mathematics to use."

The second factor moving Pauling toward biology was a certain sense of restlessness about his own work. At the age of 30, he had already studied a wide variety of inorganic molecules exhaustively. He was ready to go on to greater challenges. From the time he entered Cal Tech, he explained, he had "worked largely with inorganic substances . . . mostly rather simple substances that had ten, twenty, or thirty atoms in each molecule. But then—about 1934—I began to wonder about the large molecules in living organisms . . . protein molecules with *thousands* of atoms in them."

The first problem to which Pauling turned his attention was that of the hemoglobin molecule, the protein molecule that transports oxygen through our bloodstream. Hemoglobin is a highly complex molecule at whose core is a group of atoms known as *heme*. The "working part" of the heme group, in turn, is a single iron atom located at the group's center.

By the early 1930s, scientists were relatively certain that hemoglobin functions as a carrier of oxygen because of the ability of the iron atom in heme to bond with an oxygen atom. Some chemists believed, however, that the oxygen did not actually bind to the iron but was simply held loosely within the heme structure. Beyond these preliminary ideas, however, the exact mechanisms by which oxygen adds to and is released by hemoglobin were not well understood. Since these changes involve the formation and breaking of chemical bonds, Pauling was attracted to the problems involving hemoglobin.

In order to find out about the bonding between oxygen and hemoglobin, Pauling decided to study the electronic changes that occur in both oxygen and iron in the combined molecule (oxyhemoglobin) and its uncombined form (deoxyhemoglobin). He was assisted in this research by a graduate student, Charles Coryell.

The Quarternary Structure of Hemoglobin

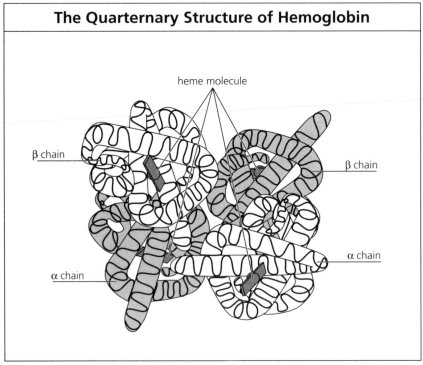

heme molecule

β chain

β chain

α chain

α chain

Figure 5

The results of the Pauling-Coryell studies were remarkable. In the first place, those experiments confirmed that oxygen actually forms a chemical bond with iron and is not just held in close association, as some chemists had believed. Far more important, however, was the discovery that the hemoglobin molecule undergoes an "extreme structural change" when it takes on or releases an oxygen molecule. Pauling and Coryell called this discovery "interesting and surprising."

The hemoglobin puzzle tickled Pauling's imagination. One result, Pauling later wrote, was that he "became interested in the general problem of the structure of proteins." It was a stroke of good fortune that this interest developed at a time when another scientist with similar interests was visiting in Pasadena.

Ava Helen with the three Pauling children, about 1934. (Courtesy of Pauling Archives; #324-36)

Alfred Mirsky, from New York City's Rockefeller Institute for Medical Research, was spending a year at Cal Tech. One of Mirsky's interests was the denaturing of protein. Denaturation is the process during which the physical properties of a protein undergo changes, often dramatic changes. During the frying of an egg, for example, the clear, colorless protein that makes up the outer portion of the egg is denatured to an opaque, white solid.

Pauling and Coryell talked with Mirsky at length about the process of denaturation. They concluded that denaturation occurs when some outside agent (such as heat, as in the frying of an egg) causes a change in the shape of protein molecules. In 1936, Pauling and Mirsky published a paper describing a chemical mechanism by which such a change might occur.

The obvious challenge that Pauling now faced was to know more about the molecular structure of proteins. Scientists had long known that proteins are complex molecules made from relatively simple building blocks, amino acids. How amino acids are arranged within a protein was not clear, however.

Some researchers argued for a *cyclol theory*, in which the amino acids are arranged in a hexagonal ring. Others believed that the amino acids are joined end-to-end in very long chains. In either case, one might then ask if a higher level of organization were also possible. Might the long chain, for example, be bent, folded, twisted, or arranged in some other shape?

In 1939, Pauling and Carl Niemann published a paper that summarized all of the evidence against the cyclol theory. That evidence was very convincing, and the cyclol theory was soon abandoned in favor of the chain model. As a result, chemists became convinced that a protein consists of a very long chain of hundreds or thousands of amino acids.

To decide what shape (or shapes) a protein molecule might take, Pauling turned to a technique with which he was familiar and comfortable, X-ray crystallography. He knew that X-ray photographs had the potential for showing precisely how amino acids are arranged in a protein. The fundamental problem was getting good diffraction patterns from protein molecules, a far more difficult problem than it was for the crystals with which Pauling had worked in the past.

At the time, the best protein diffraction patterns available were those taken by the great British crystallographer William Astbury. Astbury was employed at the University of Leeds, where he worked on the physics of textiles and fibers. Although the equipment he worked with was still somewhat primitive, his diffraction patterns provided some tantalizing clues about protein structure.

The problem was that Pauling had no success in finding a structure that would conform to Astbury's patterns. He tried to use everything he knew about chemical bonding to predict bond lengths and bond angles in the protein molecules. But none of his models fit Astbury's data.

After spending the summer of 1937 in this futile research, Pauling concluded that he was doing something wrong, that some basic assumption he was relying on must be false. He decided to try another approach to the problem. That approach was to begin studying not a complete protein itself, but a single amino acid of which proteins are made. Up to this time, no one had tried to determine the structure of a single amino acid or of a simple peptide, a compound containing two, three, or some small number of amino acids bonded to each other. In fact, Pauling's decision to study individual amino acids and small peptides was not taken seriously by other workers in the field.

To assist him in this research, Pauling turned to Robert B. Corey, who had just joined the faculty at Cal Tech. Like Mirsky, Corey had come from the Rockefeller Institute in New York City. He too was curious about the structure of proteins and agreed to begin, along the lines of Pauling's suggestion, by studying the individual amino acids and their simple compounds.

Within a year, Corey had found the structure of a dipeptide, diketopiperazine, a compound containing two amino acids joined to each other. Before long, he unraveled the structures of many of the amino acids and of some simple peptides. By 1948, the evidence from Corey's work was overwhelming. "It had become clear," Pauling wrote, "that there was nothing surprising about the dimensions of these molecules." They conformed in every way to the fundamental assumptions that Pauling had used in drawing protein structures 11 years earlier. It was not he who had been at fault, he decided. Instead, there must have been some flaw in Astbury's work.

Pauling decided to return to the task he had abandoned in 1937 and to work out a model for the structure of protein. The story of Pauling's successful solution to this puzzle is continued in Chapter Eight.

The years spent waiting for Corey's results were by no means empty ones for Pauling. In fact, as early as May 1936 he had found another topic that called for his attention, the problem of biological specificity. The occasion was a seminar given by Pauling at the Rockefeller Institute at which he discussed his research on hemoglobin. Present that day in the audience was Karl Landsteiner, Nobel Prize winner in biology in 1939 and currently on the staff at Rockefeller.

Landsteiner was intrigued by Pauling's presentation and invited Pauling to visit his laboratory so that they could talk in more detail. Landsteiner wanted to know if Pauling could explain some features of Landsteiner's current research on immunology in terms of molecular structure. Landsteiner had found that the presence of a foreign body (an antigen) in the bloodstream calls forth a very specific kind of response (an antibody) from the immune system. The response is said to be *specific* because a different antibody appears to be available for each different antigen that is known. Was there something about the molecular structures of antigen and antibody molecules, Landsteiner wondered, that would explain this specificity?

Pauling did not know the answer to this puzzle. Indeed, he was hardly aware that the phenomenon existed. But he was intrigued by the problem and decided to think more about it. Within a few days, he had read Landsteiner's book, *The Specificity of Serological Reactions*, and started to consider possible molecular explanations for Landsteiner's observations. ·

By 1939, Pauling had worked out a fundamental theory to explain these phenomena, the theory of complimentarity. According to this theory, two molecules will react with each other if their shapes allow them to approach each other very closely. In cases like those discovered by Landsteiner, an antibody can attach to an antigen, he suggested, only if the antibody molecule has a structure that will allow it to fit tightly with the antigen molecule. His paper outlining these ideas, "A Theory of the Structure and Process of Formation of Antibodies," was published in the *Journal of the American Chemical Society* in 1940.

Over the next decade, Pauling's students looked for experimental evidence to support this theory, with extraordinary success. They found that the space between an antigen and antibody molecule was often less than the diameter of an atom, showing how closely the two had approached each other. The search, Pauling said, "supported the idea of complimentarity so strongly as to require its acceptance."

Pauling soon realized that the principle of complimentarity could be applied to a wide variety of biological phenomena. Enzyme action can be explained, for example, by assuming that an enzyme molecule has a geometric shape that will allow it to approach very closely to the substrate molecule on which it acts. This kind of explanation lies at the core of one of the best-known explanations of enzyme action, the lock-and-key theory.

In a strange bit of foresight, Pauling also predicted that gene action would illustrate the principle of complimentarity. In the Sir Jesse Boot Foundation lecture at Nottingham, England, on May 28, 1948, Pauling argued that

> I believe that the genes serve as the templates on which are molded the enzymes that are responsible for the chemical characters, and that they also serve as templates for the production of replicas of themselves. . . . In general, the use of a gene or virus as a template would lead to the formation of a molecule not with identical structure but with complimentary structure.

In less than five years, Watson and Crick were to discover the structure of DNA, a molecule that has precisely the qualities described in Pauling's Boot lecture.

The late 1930s were a period of significant change in Pauling's academic career also. On June 3, 1936, A. A. Noyes died. The following year, Pauling was chosen to replace his former mentor as chairman of the Division of Chemistry and Chemical Engineering and director of the Gates Laboratory at Cal Tech. He held these positions for the next 22 years.

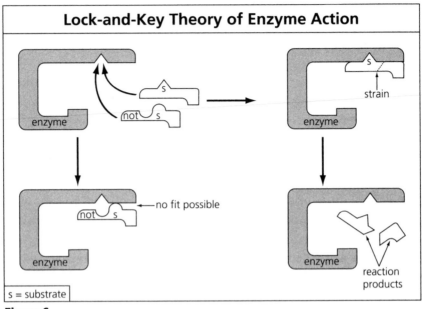

Figure 6

During the academic year 1937–38, Pauling was invited to be George Fisher Baker Lecturer at Cornell University in Ithaca, New York. These lectures, along with his earlier papers in the *Journal of the American Chemical Society*, were eventually to form the basis of his most famous book, *The Nature of the Chemical Bond*, published in 1939.

The Cornell appointment also made it possible for Pauling to continue his contacts with Karl Landsteiner. He later explained that during one visit to Ithaca Landsteiner gave him "a thorough survey of the field of serology (the study of serums used in curing disease) and [his] opinions about the reliability of some apparently contradictory experimental observations by different people." This tutorial turned out to be invaluable in Pauling's formation of the theory of complimentarity, first published two years later.

The story of Pauling's work on hemoglobin, complimentarity, and other biological phenomena stretched over a period of world-wide upheaval. Adolf Hitler's German army had invaded Austria

Pauling with Linda, about 1935. (Courtesy of Pauling Archives; #324-38)

in 1938. By 1941, the United States had been drawn into the war by the bombing of Pearl Harbor. For a half dozen years, most scientific research unrelated to military needs came to a halt. These changes affected the career of Linus Pauling as they did those of other scientists around the world.

CHAPTER 6 NOTES

p. 44   "never had a course . . . " "The Plowboy Interview: Dr. Linus Pauling," *Mother Earth News*, January/February 1978, p. 17.

p. 44   "interesting but . . . " Derek Davenport, "Vintage Pauling," *Chemtech*, December 1982, p. 715.

p. 44   "one might call . . . " Neil A. Campbell, "Crossing the Boundaries of Science," *BioScience*, December 1986, p. 738.

p. 44   "had become interested enough . . . " Linus Pauling, "Fifty Years of Progress in Structural Chemistry and Molecular Biology," *Daedalus*, Fall 1970, p. 1002.

p. 45   "he could understand . . . " Judith R. Goodstein, "Atoms, Molecules, and Linus Pauling," *Social Research*, Autumn 1984, p. 703.

p. 45   "worked largely . . . " "The Plowboy Interview," p. 17.

p. 46   "interesting and surprising . . . " Linus Pauling and Charles D. Coryell, "The Magnetic Properties and Structure of Hemoglobin, Oxyhemoglobin, and Carbon Monoxyhemoglobin," *Proceedings of the National Academy of Sciences*, April 1936, p. 213.

p. 51   "supported the idea . . . " "Fifty Years of Progress," p. 1006.

p. 51   "I believe that the genes . . . " "Fifty Years of Progress," p. 1008.

p. 52   "a thorough survey . . . " "Fifty Years of Progress," p. 1005.

7

YEARS OF TRANSITION

The 1940s were a decade of unusual upheaval for Linus Pauling, unusual even for a man whose life has always been characterized by change and evolution. Pauling's life was, of course, affected by World War II and the dramatic changes that were to follow that conflict. But it produced only a pause, and not a halt, in his ongoing research into the chemical explanations of life. In addition, Pauling began to write an entirely new chapter to his life, one that focused on politics rather than science. Finally, at the very beginning of the decade, he faced a personal medical crisis that nearly ended his life.

During the fall of 1940, Pauling began to complain of feeling unusually tired. At first, he blamed these feelings on overwork, a not-unreasonable explanation given his typical schedule of research, teaching, writing, speaking, and traveling. When his health continued to deteriorate, however, he finally agreed to see a physician. The diagnosis was not an encouraging one: glomerulonephritis. Glomerulonephritis, also known as Bright's disease, is characterized by an inflammation of the kidneys. Its cause is essentially unknown.

Although the disease can be treated today, relatively little could be done in the 1940s. Pauling was fortunate, however, to find a physician who was willing to make a major commitment of time and energy to Pauling's condition. That physician was Dr. Thomas Addis. For more than four years, Dr. Addis traveled once a week by train from Los Angeles to Pasadena to treat Pauling. Under Dr. Addis's care, Pauling slowly regained his health although he continued to experience relapses of the disease for many years.

Dr. Addis may have had an effect on Pauling that went beyond medical treatment. Addis was a Communist and had been under investigation by the federal government for his political views even before the postwar anti-Communist witch hunts. A decade after treating Pauling, Addis was to lose his job because he refused to testify before the House Un-American Activities Committee.

During his treatment, Pauling was appalled by the government's treatment of Dr. Addis. According to Pauling's biographer Anthony Serafini, "The psychological shock of witnessing the abuse, vilification, and ostracism of the man who, quite literally, had saved his life was too much for Pauling to bear." Serafini suggests that this experience may have been one of the factors involved in Linus Pauling's growing sense of political awareness.

Until the 1940s, Pauling was largely apolitical. He claims not to have voted until 1932, and when he did, he voted for Herbert Hoover. Yet, by the 1950s, Pauling was being investigated by the U.S. Congress for the revolutionary political views he held and actions he had taken. The evolution from political apathy to fervent advocacy certainly seems to require some explanation.

Probably more fundamental to this conversion than the Addis experience, however, was the influence of his wife, Ava Helen. Ava Helen had grown up in a liberal family, according to Serafini, raised by "a mother and father who were outspoken themselves and who sympathized with the poor and oppressed."

During the early years of their marriage, while Pauling was devoting himself to scientific research, Ava Helen was involved with a variety of liberal and progressive organizations and causes. These included the American Civil Liberties Union, the Women's International League for Peace, and the Pacific League, an organization later accused of being a Communist "front" committee. Serafini argues that Ava Helen's own "energy and passion" inevitably affected Pauling, who gradually became involved in political efforts similar to those supported by his wife.

Pauling himself confirms this view. His strong moral sense, he said in a 1981 interview, came from Ava Helen. "Until I was forty," he said, "I didn't take much interest in social concerns. I swallowed the argument that people in power use to suppress scientists—a scientist knows a great deal about his field but nothing

Ava Helen (second from left) at the Congress of Women of America, held in Bogotá, Colombia, July 17–22, 1970. (Courtesy of Pauling Archives; #326-17)

whatsoever about war and peace." Ava Helen's influence led him to a new view, he said. "A scientifically moral attitude has to be a world view. We have to learn to consider the whole of mankind as an organism."

Pauling's political evolution occurred slowly, over more than a decade. Besides the influence of Addis and Ava Helen, a number of specific incidents contributed to his transformation. One of these occurred in 1945. At the time, the Paulings had a nisei (second-generation Japanese) gardener working for them. The Paulings' son Peter discovered one day that someone had written "Americans die, but the Paulings hire a Jap" on their garage door in red paint. The incident was followed by other forms of harassment, such as threatening letters and telephone calls. Serafini claims that Pauling was so disturbed by this affair that "he considered a radical structuring of his life" that eventually "escalated his interest in politics."

Another factor affecting Pauling's political views was the Second World War. Prior to 1940, scientific research was largely irrelevant to the way governments conducted their businesses. Two important discoveries resulting from war research—radar and nuclear fission—were to change that equation forever. It eventually became clear that those nations with the strongest scientific establishments were to become the most powerful nations in the world.

When presented by Robert Oppenheimer with the opportunity to work on the U.S. government's Manhattan Project, the program to develop an atomic bomb, Pauling declined for reasons that he has never discussed. He did agree, however, to take part in other kinds of military research. His explanation for this deviation from his normally pacifist views was simply that "Hitler had to be stopped."

During the war years 1942–45, Pauling served his country in a number of different ways. He was a consultant to the Committee on Medical Research of the Office of Scientific Research and Development (OSRD). He also supervised a number of projects for the National Defense Research Committee of OSRD. The majority of these projects involved the development of explosive materials.

His first military contribution—an "oxygen meter"—was actually invented before the war, in 1940. The purpose of the meter was to detect the amount of oxygen remaining in a closed space as, for example, in a submarine. According to Pauling, the meter was developed in answer to requests made by all three branches of the armed forces. Its operation was based on certain magnetic properties of the oxygen atom and was eventually used on submarines and airplanes during World War II. After the war, it found applications in hospitals and in many industries. For example, it could be used to measure the amount of oxygen present in blood while a patient was being anesthetized. Pauling reported that he developed the basic idea for the device in "only three days." For his wartime contributions, Pauling was awarded the Presidential Medal for Merit in 1948 by President Harry S Truman.

The development of nuclear weapons had a particularly powerful impact on Pauling's views. Prior to, during, and after the war, he was frequently asked to talk about his area of military expertise, explosives. On one occasion, shortly after the end of the war, he was asked to compare the effects of nuclear and conventional weapons.

In preparation for the lecture, he made some calculations on this comparison and, he says, "was appalled at the magnitude of what I discovered." His rapidly growing concerns about nuclear weapons grew out of that experience and his subsequent realization that nuclear weapons "can be so destructive—and relatively cheap—that it might be difficult for power-oriented government figures to resist their use unless the world became acutely aware of the horrendous consequences."

Ultimately, Pauling took a personal vow to become more active in the anti-nuclear movement. On a boat trip to Europe in 1947, he made a "ceremonial commitment" to himself to raise the issue of world peace in every speech he made in the future, no matter what the topic.

In the postwar years, therefore, Pauling made himself available to speak about peace on many occasions. In addition, he began to make connections with other scientists who were increasingly alarmed by the possibilities of a nuclear holocaust. In 1946, for example, at the request of Albert Einstein, Pauling became a member of the Emergency Committee of Atomic Scientists. The committee, also known as the "Einstein Committee," was incorporated on August 2, 1946, for the purpose of gathering financial support for groups engaged in public education on problems of atomic energy.

When the Emergency Committee went out of business in late 1951, Pauling was very concerned. He wrote to Leo Szilard, an atomic physicist and a leader of the anti-nuclear movement, "I have been very much disturbed by the developments about atomic weapons, as described in the newspapers lately. . . . What would you think about formulating a set of questions, asking whether it would be possible to bring law and order into the world as a whole, through cooperation between the east and the west in a sincere effort to reach a peaceful solution of our problems—to achieve a permanent peace. . . . These questions would then be sent in a letter to President Truman and Premier Stalin. . . ."

Pauling's developing political consciousness did not mean that he had abandoned his scientific research. Quite the opposite. Throughout the war and in the postwar years, he managed to maintain lines of research on biological and medical topics that he had begun in the 1930s. Between 1941 and 1945, he published 34 papers on topics ranging from the crystal structure of metals to advances in resonance theory to light absorption by free radicals.

The vast majority of these papers, however, dealt with his ongoing studies of antibody-antigen reactions, originally inspired by his conversations with Karl Landsteiner. One of these papers, coauthored with Dan H. Campbell and David Pressman, described the synthesis in March 1942 of "the first synthetic antibody." Pauling's team had found a mechanism by which globulin proteins found normally in blood could be chemically altered to convert them to antibody molecules. They used these synthetic antibodies to conduct further tests on Pauling's principle of complimentarity.

The late 1940s also saw the culmination of the 11-year effort by Pauling and Robert Corey to determine the molecular structure of protein molecules. Having finally been convinced by Corey's work that his initial method of attacking this problem was correct, Pauling went back to the task of model-building.

Pauling's approach to this problem was unusual among biologists and chemists. He would use paper and pencil or Tinkertoy-like building blocks to construct a physical model of the molecule he wanted to represent. From quantum mechanics and other theoretical considerations, he knew the limitations placed on the model: bond lengths, bond angles, amount of rotation, and so on. He used great care to be sure that the models he built were precisely accurate. Once the model was constructed, he could then use it to predict experimental observations produced by the model. Those predictions could then be compared with actual data.

The breakthrough on protein structure came, interestingly enough, while Pauling was in England. In 1948, he had accepted an appointment as visiting lecturer at Balliol College in Oxford University. Shortly after his arrival, he became ill with the flu and spent a few days in bed. After a day of doing nothing other than reading detective stories, he became bored and decided that he

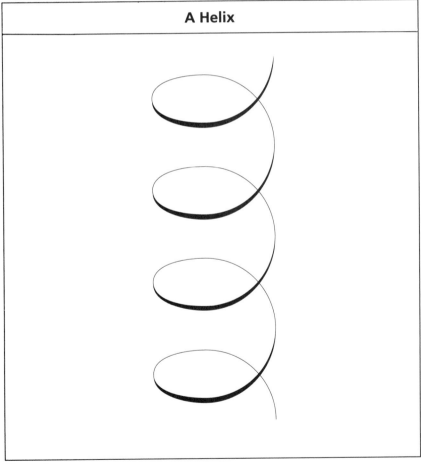

A Helix

Figure 8

should "have a crack" at unraveling the structure of the protein known as alpha keratin.

Following his usual procedure, he carefully drew out the long chain of amino acids that he knew made up the protein molecule. He then cut out the molecule, as a child might cut out a string of paper dolls. Pauling was then able to rotate, bend, and twist the molecule into shapes that it might be expected to have in nature.

After a short time, he realized that he had the answer. He arranged the protein chain in a spiral shape known as an *alpha helix* such that all bond angles and bond lengths corresponded to theoretical limitations and observed data. In addition, forces between adjacent parts of the molecule, needed to retain its shape, were immediately obvious.

Pauling did not publish his results, however, for nearly two years. The main reason for the delay was the continuing discrepancy between the pitch (distance per turn of the helix) as predicted by the model and as observed in Astbury's diffraction patterns. The difference was small—5.4 angstroms compared to 5.1 angstroms—but not insignificant. (An angstrom is a unit of length equal to one ten-billionth of a meter.)

Eventually, this discrepancy was resolved. Astbury's photographs, it turned out, were taken with protein molecules tilted slightly from the angle that would have been expected. When this correction was made, the pitch shown on his X-ray patterns was exactly what Pauling's model predicted, 5.4 angstroms.

Pauling has commented on the fact that no other researcher had been able to solve the protein structure riddle during the 11 years that Corey was working on amino acids and simple peptides. It was true that some of the world's greatest scientists were working on just this problem. At the Cavendish Laboratory in Cambridge, for example, a team of brilliant crystallographers, William Lawrence Bragg, John Kendrew, and Max Perutz had searched for clues in Astbury's photos that would lead to a model of protein structure. The Cambridge team actually published a paper on the topic a few months before Pauling and Corey's. But the Bragg-Kendrew-Perutz paper was "long, diffuse, uncharacteristically uncertain, an illustrated mail-order catalog of the latest polypeptide models." It did

Pauling with a model of the alpha helix. (Courtesy of Pauling Archives; #324-109)

not specifically suggest any one model as the most likely structure for proteins.

Pauling's explanation for the failure of others to solve this puzzle provides insight into his own genius. Protein researchers had long assumed that in any helical model, there would have to be an integral number of amino acids in a complete turn of the helix. That is, if you started at one amino acid in the helix and traveled up and along the helix until you were exactly above that amino acid, you would have had to travel through two, three, four, or some other exact number of amino acids, never through 2.3, 3.7, 4.1, or some other fractional number. Pauling pointed out that there was really no reason to make that assumption. Indeed, his own model contained 3.61 amino acid groups per turn of the helix. And once the possibility of fractional values is accepted, the model works out totally satisfactorily.

The first report of the helical structure of protein molecules was published in a 1951 paper in the *Proceedings of the National Academy of Sciences.* Over the next year, Pauling and Corey published a dozen more papers on the structure of proteins found in hair, muscle, feathers, hemoglobin, and related proteins. Included among these papers was the report of a second structure discovered for protein molecules, a shape known as a *pleated sheet.* This shape, similar to the middle layer of corrugated cardboard, was found to exist in certain types of protein that did not assume the helical pattern.

Pauling's work on the structure of protein molecules had led him in a second direction at about the same time, a study of the geometry of nucleic acid molecules. One of the most fundamental questions in biology during the 20th century was how genetic information is stored in cells. The pioneering research of Gregor Mendel in the mid-1800s had led to a number of quantitative rules describing the pattern in which hereditary traits are passed from one generation to the next. Those rules suggested the existence of certain discrete units that carry genetic information. But no one knew exactly what these units were. At various times, the units were given names such as *biophore, gemmule, pangene,* and—eventually—*gene.* Naming this unit of hereditary information did not mean, however, that scientists knew what it was.

During the 1930s and 1940s, discussions centered on the possibility that either protein molecules or molecules of nucleic acid might somehow be capable of storing genetic information. The two research teams that best understood this challenge were Pauling and his coworkers at Cal Tech and James Watson and Francis Crick at the Cavendish. Both groups assumed that the arrangement of atoms in molecules provided a mechanism for storing genetic information.

The puzzle was eventually solved by Watson and Crick in 1953 when they discovered the double helical structure of deoxyribonucleic acid (DNA). Almost to the very end of their search, however, Watson and Crick worried that Pauling would find the answer before them. They knew that Pauling had been working on the structure of DNA for some time, and they feared that he would get the correct structure first.

Their fears were well based. Pauling had started working on the structure of DNA in 1948 when he became convinced that DNA was the carrier of genetic information. All he had to work with, however, were some poor quality diffraction photos produced by Astbury and I. O. Bell in 1938 and some "equally poor photographs" taken at Cal Tech.

Pauling knew by 1951 of better DNA photographs, those taken by Maurice Wilkins and Rosalind Franklin at King's College, London, but he was unable to get copies of the photographs. Wilkins claimed that "he had not reached the stage when he wished to show them." Pauling was thus prevented from seeing the latest and best set of photographs that would almost certainly have been the key he needed to solve the DNA puzzle.

In one of the great ironies of the history of science, Pauling probably would have been able to view the photographs had he been allowed to attend the protein meeting scheduled for April 28, 1952, in England (see Chapter 1). Historians are convinced that, had Pauling been at the conference, Wilkins would have shown him at least some of the work being done in his laboratories.

Instead, it was James Watson who saw and first realized the significance of the King's College photographs. In his book telling about the search for the structure of DNA, Watson describes his reaction to seeing Franklin's famous "photograph 51." "The instant I saw the picture," he writes, "my mouth fell open and my pulse began to race." Watson could see at a glance that photograph 51 contained the answer for which he, Crick, and Pauling were all looking.

Knowing that the answer was there and finding the answer were, however, two different things. Watson and Crick still had a lot of hard work ahead of them. And they were fully aware of Pauling's genius and his earlier success with the structure of the protein molecule. Would he win this race with the Cavendish researchers, as he had the protein contest?

Their fears were heightened when, in January of 1953, they learned that Pauling and Corey had submitted a paper to *The Proceedings of the National Academy of Sciences* proposing a structure for the DNA molecule. The bearer of this news was Pauling's son Peter, who was by coincidence also working in Cambridge at the time. It was with real concern, therefore, that they

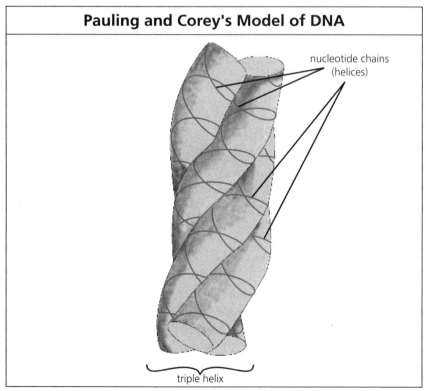

Pauling and Corey's Model of DNA

nucleotide chains (helices)

triple helix

Figure 7

accepted from Peter on January 28 a copy of the paper his father had just sent him.

Within moments, however, their fears turned to elation. The triple helix structure proposed by Pauling and Corey could not possibly be correct. Pauling had made a number of errors that were immediately obvious to Watson and Crick. They could scarcely believe that someone of Pauling's stature could have gone so far wrong. "If a student had made a similar mistake," Watson later wrote, "he would be thought unfit to benefit from Cal Tech's chemistry department [where Pauling was a professor]."

The point of this episode, of course, is that even geniuses are not perfect. Like any other great scientist, Pauling made errors as well as brilliant discoveries. The big difference in Pauling's case, however, has been pointed out by one of his colleagues. "Linus's bad ideas," James Bonner has said, "are better than most people's good ones."

Pauling's anger at having been refused a passport in 1952 did not disappear quickly. He had looked forward to debating the topic of protein structure with the greatest scientists in the world. Finally he determined that, if he couldn't go to the conference, the conference would have to come to him. As a result, he scheduled a second conference on protein structure, this one to be held at Cal Tech in September 1953.

Almost the entire cast of characters involved in the original London conference and, later, in the DNA race showed up in Pasadena, Watson, Crick, Bragg, Perutz, Kendrew, and Wilkins among them. The presentations were long and the debates exciting, but there seemed to be little controversy over the alpha helix. Serafini suggests that the reason for the unanimity of opinion may have been that "Perutz, the dean of British protein scientists, had come to the conclusion that Pauling was right and that the alpha-helix was correct."

Pauling experienced much greater success with another line of research that began somewhat earlier than his DNA studies. At a 1945 meeting of the Century Club in New York City, Pauling first heard about some studies then being conducted on sickle-cell anemia. Sickle-cell anemia is a disease in which a person's red blood cells become deformed and lose their ability to carry oxygen efficiently. The disease is often very painful and frequently results in death.

It occurred to Pauling that, rather than being a problem of red blood cells themselves, sickle-cell anemia might be caused by an abnormality in hemoglobin molecules found in the red blood cells. Such an abnormality might, he thought, prevent hemoglobin molecules from bonding properly to oxygen molecules.

Pauling's interest in sickle-cell anemia was natural enough. He had been studying hemoglobin on and off for more than a decade. And he saw in sickle-cell anemia a condition that might be explained using his principle of complimentarity. "I thought at

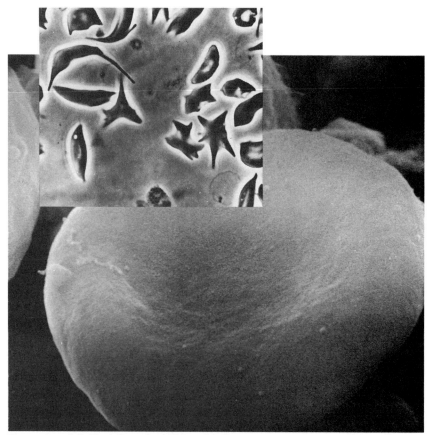

Normal and sickled (inset) red blood cells. (Courtesy of National Institutes of Health)

once," he has written, "that the abnormal hemoglobin molecules that I postulated to be present in the red cells of these patients would have two mutually complimentary regions on their surfaces, such as to cause them to aggregate into long columns."

To confirm his suspicions, Pauling asked one of his graduate students, Dr. Harvey Itano, to do a comparative analysis of the blood of sickle-cell patients and normal individuals. Dr. Itano had already earned his M.D. degree and was then studying with Pauling for a Ph.D. in chemistry.

Pauling's assignment was a technically difficult one. A technique for analyzing a mixture of proteins such as those in blood—electrophoresis—had only recently been developed by the Swedish chemist Arne Wilhelm Tiselius. Dr. Itano and an assistant, S. J. Singer, spent more than three years unraveling the puzzle of abnormal hemoglobin molecules. They were eventually able to show that such molecules differ from normal hemoglobin molecules in a surprisingly modest way. One of the amino acids they contain (out of a total of 146) is incorrect. This single error is sufficient to alter hemoglobin and reduce its ability to transport oxygen. The report of this discovery was carried in the journal *Science* in a 1949 paper entitled "Sickle-cell Anemia, a Molecular Disease." Pauling later commented that, to his knowledge, it was the first time that the term *molecular disease* had been used.

The postwar years marked a period in which Pauling's international reputation was solidified. He was awarded with a series of honors and prizes that are reserved for only the most highly respected members of the chemical profession. Among these were the J. Willard Gibbs Medal of the Chicago Section of the American Chemical Society (ACS; 1946), appointment as Silliman Lecturer at Yale University (1947), the Theodore William Richards Medal of the Northeast Section of the ACS, the Davy Medal of the Royal Society in London (1947), and the Gilbert Newton Lewis Medal of the California Section of the ACS (1951). In addition, he was elected president of the American Chemical Society in 1949. He was also awarded honorary doctorates by a number of institutions, including Oxford and the University of Paris (both in 1948).

In addition, Pauling continued to publish prolifically. The number of scientific papers had reached 200 by 1948. He also added two more books to his list of credits. Pauling had been thinking about writing textbooks for beginning chemistry students as early as 1933. In that year, he began work on "a high school chemistry book based on structural chemistry," a book that was never actually published. When he started teaching freshman chemistry at Cal Tech in 1937, he could not find a book that he liked, so decided to write his own. That book finally came out in 1947 as *General Chemistry: An Introduction to Descriptive Chemistry and Modern Chemical Theory*. Pauling is reported to have asked W. H. Freeman of San Francisco to publish the book in order to "help West Coast publishers." *General Chemistry* was eventually translated into French, Spanish, Indian, German, Gujurati, Hebrew, Japanese, Portuguese, and Roumanian. Three years later, Freeman published a second introductory text by Pauling, *College Chemistry*. It was eventually translated into Hindi and Japanese.

The end of World War II had allowed Pauling to return to his scientific pursuits. But he was never again to be "only" a scientist. As the 1950s dawned, he found himself more fully embroiled in political issues. As he reached the peak of his scientific career, he also opened a new chapter as an important spokesman for some of the most critical social, ethical, and political issues of the day.

CHAPTER 7 NOTES

p. 56   "The psychological shock . . . " Anthony Serafini, *Linus Pauling: A Man and His Science* (New York: Paragon House, 1989), p. 110.

p. 56   "a mother and father . . . " Serafini, p. 107.

p. 56   "Until I was forty . . . " Carol Pogash, "The Great Gadfly," *Science Digest*, June 1981, p. 91.

p. 58   "he considered . . . " Serafini, p. 111.

p. 58   "Hitler . . . " John Hogan, "Profile: Linus C. Pauling," *Scientific American*, March 1993, p. 40.

p. 59   "was appalled . . . " William F. Fry, Jr., "What's New with You, Linus Pauling?" *The Humanist*, November/December 1974, p. 17.

p. 65   "he had not reached . . . " Linus Pauling, "Fifty Years of Progress in Structural Chemistry and Molecular Biology," *Daedalus*, Fall 1970, p. 1009.

p. 65   "The instant . . . " James Watson, *The Double Helix* (New York: Atheneum Press, 1968), p. 167.

p. 67   "If a student . . . " Watson, p. 161.

p. 67   "Linus's bad ideas . . . " As quoted in Serafini, p. 101.

p. 67   "Perutz, the dean . . . " Serafini, p. 154.

p. 68   "I thought at once . . . " "Fifty Years of Progress," p. 1011.

p. 70   "help West Coast . . . " Clifford S. Mead, ed., *The Pauling Catalogue* (Corvallis: Oregon State University, 1991), p. xv.

8

FROM NOBEL PRIZE TO NOBEL PRIZE

Wednesday morning, November 3, 1954, began like many other autumn mornings in Ithaca, New York. Linus Pauling was preparing to give a lecture on hemoglobin to a group of undergraduate and graduate students at Cornell University. Only a few hours later, there was no longer anything ordinary or routine about the day. In the midst of his lecture, Pauling was called to the telephone where he received word that he had just been awarded the 1954 Nobel Prize in chemistry.

The Nobel citation explained that Pauling was being honored "for his research into the nature of the chemical bond and its application to the structure of complex substances." Unsurprisingly, Pauling was thrilled with his award and the check for $35,066 that went with it. The Nobel Prize is the highest honor any scientist can receive, a recognition of some great accomplishment in the sciences. Pauling's office was flooded with congratulatory messages from around the world.

Yet long before 1954, Pauling had turned his attention to other issues that seemed more important, issues of war and peace, of life and death. His concern about these issues grew out of his belief in pacifism and a general distaste for violence, as well as more specific worries about the growing threat of nuclear weapons. It was his view that nuclear weapons posed a real and substantial threat to all of humanity. He argued that a battle to see who could build the largest weapons and the greatest number of them would inevitably lead to a horrible holocaust. He called for the nations of the world to insure peace, not by an arms race, but by forming relationships among themselves.

Linus and Ava Helen after hearing about Pauling's Nobel Prize in chemistry, November 1954. (Courtesy of Pauling Archives, #324-82)

In a 1950 speech at Carnegie Hall, he explained: "It is not necessary that the social and economic system in Russia be identical with that in the United States in order that these two great nations can be at peace with one another. It is only necessary that the people of the United States and the people of Russia should have respect for one another, a deep desire to work for progress and a mutual recognition that war has finally ruled itself out as the arbitration of the destiny of humanity."

Pauling was by no means the only scientist arguing this position in the postwar world. Indeed, the number of scientists who pushed *for* weapons development was relatively small. Virtually all of the great names in science who had worked on the Manhattan Project—Leo Szilard, Robert Oppenheimer, Hans Bethe, Harold Urey, Eugene Wigner, Enrico Fermi, and Eugene Rabinowitch, to name only a few—were horrified at the prospect of a spreading nuclear arsenal in the United States and other nations of the world.

Pauling began to speak out almost as soon as the war ended. As a member of the Research Board for National Security from 1945 to 1946, he took pains to point out the dangers of nuclear conflict. In a 1947 speech, three years before the first hydrogen bomb was tested, he warned that the bomb might "have a destructive effect, a hundred, a thousand, nay ten thousand times greater than the bombs dropped on Hiroshima and Nagasaki."

An important event in his evolution as an anti-war advocate appears to have been a 1950 meeting with Albert Einstein. In a letter to Leo Szilard describing that meeting, Pauling declared that "the question of peace or war has now become so important as to overshadow all other questions—it is of a far greater order of magnitude that anything else."

Pauling's opinions and activities did not escape the attention of the vigorous anti-Communist movement that swept the United States in the early 1950s. Inspired and led by Wisconsin Senator Joe McCarthy, politicians and legislators at every governmental level set out to find and punish anyone who was suspected of having Communist sympathies. The movement spread like wildfire, eventually resulting in the dismissal and/or public humiliation of thousands of American citizens, many of whom had committed no crime other than expressing unpopular political views.

Senator McCarthy clearly felt that Pauling was not to be trusted. He was quoted as saying that the Nobel Prize winner had "a well-nigh incredible record of membership in Communist-front organizations." To be sure, both Linus and Ava Helen had been members of progressive organizations, but neither had ever been a Communist. Pauling declared openly that he was "not even a theoretical Marxist."

McCarthy's opinion was apparently strongly influenced by the testimony of one Louis Budenz, a faculty member at Fordham University and a self-acknowledged Communist. Budenz had accused Pauling of being a member of "a group of alleged Communists," a charge that Pauling rejected as "a lie."

Suspicions about Pauling's loyalty were especially pronounced in his home state of California, where McCarthyism was probably stronger than anywhere else in the nation. On November 14, 1950, Pauling announced that he had been called to testify before the Senate Investigating Committee on Education. The main topic of the hearing was Pauling's objection to loyalty oaths.

Loyalty oaths were special pledges that were being demanded of workers in many public and private organizations. They required workers to swear that they were not Communists and did not support Communist organizations, activities, or ideas. Anyone who refused to sign a loyalty oath was subject to dismissal.

Pauling's position on this issue was clear. He felt that governmental bodies had no business inquiring into the political beliefs of individual citizens. He had no intention of cooperating with legislative committees that wanted to know about his own political attitudes or those of colleagues. When he was called to testify before a committee of the U.S. Senate some years later, he made this position clear. "I believe," he said, "that the Senate Internal Security Subcommittee has misused its authority in its harassment of me and other loyal Americans who have not been guilty of any illegal action but have striven to do their duty as citizens. . . . Senator Dodd is carrying out his attacks on the peace movement in the United States by suppressing free speech and free discussions."

Still, Pauling was always perfectly willing to express his political viewpoints *outside* of legislative halls. On many occasions, he made it clear to the public that he was not a Communist, nor did he endorse a Communist philosophy. Upon receiving the subpoena from the California investigating committee, for example, Pauling tried to make his position clear. In a statement released to the press at the time, he announced: "I am not a Communist. I have never been a Communist. I have never been involved with the Communist Party."

A decade later, before Senator Dodd's Senate subcommittee, he was still making the same point. "I have not served Communist causes and objectives," he said, "and I am indignant that your Subcommittee should accuse me of doing so."

Pauling's refusal to cooperate wholeheartedly with various legislative committees annoyed colleagues, a few friends, and a number of Cal Tech trustees. The tenor of the time was such that anyone who refused to take a loyalty oath—for whatever reason—was largely assumed to be a Communist or Communist sympathizer. Little or no effort was made to distinguish between those who might actually have fit that description and those who had honest reservations about the propriety of even requiring such an oath.

The question soon arose at Cal Tech, therefore, as to what should "be done" about Pauling. Some colleagues thought his presence on campus brought disgrace to the institution and wanted him to leave. And a group of trustees made an effort to remove Pauling from his professorship. In the end, no action was taken, and Pauling was retained. The long-term effects of this controversy were another matter. According to biographer Anthony Serafini, Pauling's prestige was seriously damaged and "he never again held the exalted position he was used to at Cal Tech."

Pauling was having his problems at the federal level also. His application for a passport to attend the April 1952 protein conference in England (see Chapter 1) was denied first by the chief of the Passport Division of the State Department, Ruth Shipley, and then again by her immediate superior, S. D. Boykin, director of the Office of Security and Consular Affairs at the State Department. The final denial by Boykin came even after Pauling had submitted statements made under oath that he was not then and had never been a Communist or Communist sympathizer. The State Department said it acted to deny the passport because Pauling's "anti-Communist statements were not sufficiently strong."

The U.S. government's actions in this affair evoked a nearly unanimous and vigorous response from scientists around the world. Even colleagues with whom Pauling had disagreed in the past wrote President Truman and secretary of state Dean Acheson to express their outrage. Albert Einstein argued that the government's action was "seriously detrimental to the interest and reputation of this country." Another letter signed by Enrico Fermi, Harold Urey, and Edward Teller, among others, said, "We cannot believe, with the greatest stretch of our imagination, that any reason can exist which would make the granting of a passport [to Pauling] of so great harm to this country as its withdrawal"

The barrage of letters apparently had some effect. Pauling applied one more time for a passport and, in August, received one good for limited travel. The passport was good for only two months, instead of the usual five years. Of course, the passport came much too late to allow him to attend the protein conference. But, he and Ava Helen went abroad anyway, spending six weeks in England and Paris during which time Pauling attended the Second International Congress of Biochemistry in Paris and a meeting of the Faraday Society on the physical chemistry of proteins in London.

Pauling continued to have passport problems in 1953 and 1954. The first occurred when he was asked to lay a cornerstone in honor of Chaim Weizmann at the Institute of Science in Tel Aviv named in honor of Israel's famous scientist and first president. Pauling was granted a passport, but it was good for only the single trip to Israel and back, and for no other travel. The second event involved Pauling's request for a passport in July of 1954 that would have allowed him to attend, at Prime Minister Nehru's special invitation, the dedication of a scientific institution in India. On this occasion, he was refused even a limited passport.

As disappointing as these rejections and limited victories were, they were not nearly as serious as was the third case that occurred a few months later in November of 1954. This time, Pauling requested a passport so that he would be able to travel to Sweden and accept his Nobel Prize in chemistry. Although he made his request as soon as he heard of the award, the passport office did not respond for over three weeks. It appeared that his unpopular political views would once more prevent his traveling abroad, this time for a far more important event than was the case in 1952.

Passport officials were clearly feeling pressures from conservative politicians. Senator T. C. Hennings, Jr., of Missouri complained to the State Department, asking whether it was "allowing some groups of people in some foreign country to determine which Americans get passports?"

But scientists from around the world were making their views known too. The embarrassment that would have resulted from denying Pauling's request yet again eventually became obvious, and he received his passport on November 27, 1954. That left the Paulings just enough time to pack and get to Stockholm for the Nobel ceremonies on December 9.

During the second half of the 1950s, the cold war between the United States and the Soviet Union heated up . . . and so did Pauling's campaign against nuclear weapons. On July 15, 1955, for example, along with 52 other Nobel Prize winners, he signed the Mainau Declaration calling for an end to all war, especially nuclear war. The Mainau Declaration began by acknowledging that nuclear weapons had thus far been a strong deterrent to warfare. But, the signers went on to say, "we think it is a delusion if governments believe that they can avoid war for a long time through the fear of these weapons. Fear and tension have often engendered wars. . . . All nations must come to the decision to renounce force as a final resort of policy. If they are not prepared to do this, they will cease to exist."

In 1957, Pauling helped establish the Pugwash Movement for Science and World Affairs, an organization named after its meeting location, Pugwash, Nova Scotia, and its objective, an effort to promote the signing of a nuclear test ban treaty.

Pauling also began to talk and write about the biological effects of radioactive fallout. Beginning in the mid-1950s, the United States and the Soviet Union tested dozens of nuclear devices by exploding them in the atmosphere. The purpose of these tests was to determine the effectiveness of weapons being developed by each nation. One terrible side-effect of the tests, however, was the release of large amounts of dangerously radioactive materials into the atmosphere. After a certain period of time—ranging from a few hours to a few months—these materials settled back to Earth where they contaminated soil, plants, and water supplies. Some scientists, Pauling included, became concerned about the possible health effects of this nuclear fallout on the health of humans. He tried to calculate the effects on the human body and genes that might result from increasing levels of radioactive isotopes such as strontium-90 and carbon-14 in the atmosphere. His first presentation on this topic, "Health Hazards of Radiation," was presented before the California Division of the American Cancer Society on October 3, 1957. He followed that presentation with more articles in professional journals and, increasingly, in popular publications. His article, "Why Every Test Kills," in *Liberation* (February 1958) and his letter, "Genetic Menace of Tests," in the *New York Times* (May 1958) are examples of the latter.

Richard S. Lewis, former editor of the *Bulletin of the Atomic Scientists*, credits Pauling for being "one of the first to suggest the long-term dangers of low-level radiation. I recall hearing him at lectures," Lewis says, "when he projected, with great logic and persuasiveness, the hazards of this form of radiation."

Not all scientists agreed with Pauling on this point. In fact, the U.S. government's official position was that nuclear testing and the fallout it produced posed essentially no harm to human health. A member of the Atomic Energy Commission (AEC), Dr. Willard Libby, had announced in 1954 that the amount of fallout "could be increased 15,000 times without hazard." Libby, a highly respected chemist, had devised the method of radioactive carbon dating in the mid-1940s and was to win the 1960 Nobel Prize in chemistry for this discovery.

More to the point for many observers was the cost of *not* testing. If the United States were to fall behind in the arms race, they felt, the likelihood of a nuclear war would probably increase. The number of lives that would be lost in such a war, these people felt, would be far greater than those threatened by fallout from testing.

As a matter of fact, the scientific evidence then available on this point was unclear at the time. The effects of high levels of radiation—radiation sickness and death—were already known as a result of the bomb blasts at Hiroshima and Nagasaki. But it was to be much more difficult to estimate long-term carcinogenic (cancer-causing) and genetic effects from levels of radiation so low that they produced no immediate, observable results. Indeed, dispute remains today as to how those effects can be reliably quantified.

But nuclear testing was gradually becoming more of a political than purely scientific issue for Pauling. In spite of uncertainties remaining about the biological effects of radiation, he began to move politically to get the United States and the Soviet Union to sign a ban on the testing of nuclear weapons.

An important event in this evolution occurred in May 1957. During a speech on "Science in the Modern World" at Washington University in St. Louis, Pauling recited his vision of a nuclear holocaust. At one point in his speech, he passionately proclaimed that "no human being should be sacrificed . . . to the project of perfecting nuclear weapons that could kill hundreds of millions of human beings, could devastate this beautiful world in which we live." The response of his audience was overwhelming. According to Serafini, "the audience cheered him and applauded wildly."

Immediately after the speech, Pauling met with two of his colleagues, Barry Commoner and Edward Condon, to talk about the event. Commoner was a biologist who was to become one of the most articulate spokesmen for the environment during the 1960s and 1970s. Condon was a nuclear physicist who had long worked on nuclear fission and weapons research. The trio decided to initiate an all-out effort to influence U.S. policy on the testing of nuclear arms by distributing a petition to colleagues throughout the world. The petition was later to become known as the Pauling Appeal. Pauling, Commoner, and Condon worked most of the night writing the petition and began to circulate it immediately.

The petition said, in part, "We have in common with our fellow men a deep concern for the welfare of all human beings. As scientists, we have knowledge of the dangers involved and therefore a special responsibility to make those dangers known. We deem it imperative that immediate action be taken to effect an international agreement to stop the testing of all nuclear weapons."

The petition drive was immediately successful. Within a month, more than 2,500 American scientists alone had returned signed copies. Among the original signers were 36 Nobel laureates, including eight in physics, 12 in chemistry, 13 in physiology or medicine, Bertrand Russell (in literature), Albert Schweitzer (peace), and Lord Boyd Orr (peace).

This response encouraged Pauling to write President Eisenhower on June 4, 1957, sending him a copy of the petition and outlining the potential biological and genetic hazards of continued testing of nuclear weapons. He concluded by offering to come to Washington "to answer whatever questions you wish to ask me."

Pauling's letter had little effect. The president's assistant, Sherman Adams, responded on June 29, 1957, that "extensive hearings on the subject before a committee of the Congress, by scientists who appeared as witnesses, are reported to have shown little or no uniformity of opinion."

The fact is that Pauling did not have unanimous support among scientists, and powerful political forces were aligned against him. Typical of scientific doubts were those of Eugene Rabinowitch, editor of *The Bulletin of the Atomic Scientists.* Rabinowitch wrote Pauling that he had no reasons to doubt the more conservative position on fallout taken by Libby and the AEC. He was not able, therefore, to sign the Pauling Appeal.

Rabinowitch's position was an intriguing one. He was one of the leading advocates of controls on nuclear weapons. Indeed, *The Bulletin of the Atomic Scientists* was and continues to be the primary journal through which opponents of nuclear weapons express their views. Rabinowitch's argument was, however, that nuclear technology was here to stay, and the world would just have to learn how to live with it. "The effort to end nuclear testing," he wrote, "is the expression of an unfounded belief in the possibility of reversing the advancement of military technology which has occurred since 1945."

Political opposition to Pauling was based largely on suppositions that he was a Communist or Communist sympathizer. He was never to free himself—and especially not during this period—of charges that his peace efforts were somehow aimed at undermining the U.S. government.

At the very least, scientists who supported a test ban were often considered "out of their depths." They might be geniuses in their own fields of biology, chemistry, or physics, but they just didn't understand the workings of politics and international diplomacy. The columnist Fulton Lewis, Jr., for example, wrote of Pauling and the petition signers that they were "the naive, unworldly, politically immature type who refuse to recognize the Machiavellian nature and machinations of the Communist conspiracy."

Pauling was not dissuaded from his efforts, however, and he continued to circulate his petition. Finally, on January 15, 1958, he submitted the petition, signed by 11,021 scientists from 49 nations, to Dag Hammarskjöld, secretary general of the United Nations.

Shortly thereafter, the debate over nuclear weapons testing found a more personal expression. On February 21, 1958, Pauling took part in a debate with Edward Teller on San Francisco's public television station, KQED. Teller, a Hungarian-born refugee from German oppression, had immigrated to the United States in 1935. He was, and still is, a brilliant physicist and ardent advocate of nuclear weapons. His espousal of fusion weapons in the 1940s and 1950s earned him the title "Father of the Hydrogen Bomb."

Debate between Pauling (left) and Edward Teller (right), February 21, 1948. (Courtesy of Pauling Archives; #324-111)

In the late 1950s, Teller was perhaps the most outspoken opponent of a nuclear weapons test ban treaty. In articles, speeches, and testimony before legislative bodies, Teller pleaded for a continuation of weapons development. His argument was that any health problems associated with the testing of weapons were well worth the risk compared to the far more serious dangers of falling behind the Soviet Union in an arms race.

In his debate with Pauling, Teller argued that there was no strong evidence for carcinogenic and genetic effects of radiation. "This alleged damage which the small radioactivity from the testing of nuclear weapons is causing—supposedly cancer and leukemia—has not been proved, to the best of my knowledge, by any kind of decent and clear statistics. It is possible that there *is* damage. It is even possible, to my mind, that there is *no damage*; and there is the possibility, furthermore, that very small amounts of radioactivity are helpful." Teller then went on to make the point that dangers of radiation from a war would be far worse than any possible dangers from fallout.

Pauling responded by arguing that ". . . according to the best estimates of geneticists, all of whom agree, fifteen thousand children are sacrificed for every large bomb tested. . . . " Pauling then concluded his argument with the view that "We believe as individuals that we should obey the commandment 'Thou Shalt Not Kill.' The time has come now for nations, too, to accept this commandment."

For some years, Pauling had also been working on a more formal presentation of his views, a book called *No More War!* In the book, published in 1958, Pauling presented an extreme pacifist view, arguing that virtually no war is morally acceptable. The only exception, he believed, was wars in which people rose up to liberate themselves from a tyrannical government.

In the first part of the book, Pauling summarizes all of the reasons that nuclear war must be prevented at all costs. He then goes on to outline the methods by which war can be eliminated. He proposes a World Peace Organization, under the auspices of the United Nations, through which scholars from around the world could develop methods for the advancement of peaceful resolution of conflicts. He also suggests that the United States add a secretary of peace to the president's cabinet.

Pauling's book had relatively little effect on politicians or scientists. Most seemed to feel that, as admirable as its intent may have been, it was too unrealistic. Pauling's personal appeals to President Eisenhower, colleagues, and personal friends came to naught, and he returned to other forms of political activism to advance his ideas.

One of the most dramatic of these was Pauling's legal action against the U.S. government. In 1958, he had come to the conclusion that court action might be an effective way to bring about the end of nuclear weapons testing. He thought that "suits to seek to enjoin responsible officials in the USSR, Great Britain and the United States from further detonation of those weapons" [should] be explored.

As a result, Pauling, a number of peace activists, and a group of Japanese fishermen filed suit on April 4, 1958, in the District Court of Washington, D.C., naming Secretary of Defense Neil McElroy and members of the Atomic Energy Commission as defendants. The suit said, in part, "The defendants' past and threatened future acts of exploding nuclear weapons did and will cause the plaintiffs to be damaged genetically and somatically, will cause their progeny to be deleteriously affected because of the additional radiation brought about by the acts of the defendants, and, with high probability, did and will cause the plaintiffs to suffer various diseases which they would not suffer but for the additional radiation brought about by the acts of the defendants."

The suit eventually worked its way to the Supreme Court, which refused to hear it. Although no decision was reached on the case, it generated a great deal of publicity in the popular press for the anti-nuclear—and Pauling's—case against weapons testing.

In some respects, Pauling's efforts—his United Nations' petition, *No More War!*, and the court action, for example—appeared to be without effect. Yet, the constant barrage of criticism may well have been having subtle effects on public opinion and on the attitudes of governments. As one indication, the Soviet Union, the United States, and Great Britain all decided in 1958, without signing any formal agreement, to stop the testing of nuclear weapons in the atmosphere.

Whatever influence Pauling may have had in bringing about the cessation of testing, he was still regarded as a pariah by many American legislative leaders. He was reminded of that fact in stark terms in June of 1960 when he was subpoenaed to appear before the Senate Internal Security Committee. The committee was still trying to flush out Communists and Communist sympathizers, looking this time for those who might have infiltrated the campaign against nuclear weapons. "The decision to request Dr. Pauling's testimony," the committee report explained, "was reached as a result of newly available information, including evidence of serious Communist infiltration in the various movements urging a nuclear test ban."

In particular, the committee wanted to know more about Pauling's peace petition. Senator Thomas Dodd of Connecticut explained, "Our interest in Dr. Pauling's petition is justified by Dr. Pauling's own record of service to Communist causes and objectives, many of them related in no way to his special field of science."

The committee intended to ask Pauling to testify "with respect to Communist participation in, or support of, a propaganda campaign against nuclear testing, and other Communists or Communist-front activity with respect to which you may have knowledge."

Pauling was, not surprisingly, furious at yet another attempt to stop his anti-war actions. "No one tells me what to do," he said some years later about the incident. "I make up my own mind."

Pauling tried to go part way in meeting the committee's demands. He gave committee members the list of petition signers, his own press releases about the petition, a history of how the petition developed, a financial accounting, and a list of people to whom he had written asking for help in the petition. What he refused to do was to name those individuals who had actually obtained signatures for the petition. He based this decision on the fear that anyone he named would, like himself, be subjected to harassment by the committee. More generally, he believed that the committee had exceeded its constitutional bounds and told the members that they had no right to ask for further information.

The committee adjourned, instructing Pauling to appear again on August 9, this time with *all* the information it had asked for. Pauling immediately presented his case to the courts, in a suit to prevent the committee from continuing its investigation of him, and to the general public, in a series of press releases, speeches, and articles about the hearings.

Pauling's legal action against the committee was unsuccessful, but he was able to postpone his next appearance for a number of months. Most observers thought that his appearance, finally scheduled for October 11, would "provide a dramatic showdown and would generate a legal controversy of considerable importance." In fact, the hearing turned out to be "something of a dud."

Pauling and committee members sparred back and forth for the better part of the day, but he continued to refuse to give the names of those who had assisted him. Instead of citing him for contempt, as it was clearly capable of doing, the committee retreated. Senator Dodd, chairing the meeting, simply said "very well" to Pauling's final refusal, and the matter was dropped.

The government's ongoing harassment of Pauling did not slow his anti-war activities. At the conclusion of the Internal Security Committee hearings, he began work on another petition, this one aimed at stopping the spread of nuclear weapons. It said, in part,

> We, the men and women whose names are signed below, believe that stockpiles of nuclear weapons should not be allowed to spread to any more nations or groups of nations. . . . We accordingly urge that the present nuclear powers not transfer nuclear weapons to other nations or groups of nations such as the North Atlantic Treaty Organization or the Warsaw Pact group, that all nations not now possessing these weapons voluntarily refrain from obtaining or developing them, and that the United Nations and all nations increase their efforts to achieve total and universal disarmament. . . .

At about the same time, Linus and Ava Helen began to plan for an international peace conference in Oslo, Norway, to be held May 2, 1961. The aim of the conference, according to Pauling, was to prevent the United States and the Soviet Union from providing nuclear weapons to their allies in the North Atlantic Treaty Organization and the Warsaw Pact, respectively. Such a move, Pauling noted in his opening address to the conference, "would surely

Ava Helen speaking at a peace rally in San Francisco. (Courtesy of Pauling Archives #324-136)

increase the danger of war." Ava Helen was actively involved in the planning and conduct of the conference. In her address to the conference, she said that the 60-odd delegates from a dozen nations were "working to save humanity itself."

Ever the master of public relations maneuvers, Pauling was constantly looking for ways to bring his case before the public. For example, President John F. Kennedy invited all Nobel Prize laureates from the United States to a dinner at the White House on the evening of April 29, 1962. Pauling accepted the invitation, but before going in to dinner, spent some time walking a picket line that had been set up outside the White House by a group of peace activists. His sister-in-law later expressed the view "That takes some guts; but that was Linus; if he felt like doing something he went ahead and did it."

No one can measure exactly how and to what extent Linus Pauling's peace efforts eventually influenced the actions of the United States and other governments. At least one group was convinced, however, that those efforts had been significant. On

Pauling at a White House protest, April 29, 1962. (Courtesy of Mrs. Linda Kamb)

October 10, 1963, the announcement was made that Pauling had been awarded the Nobel Peace Prize.

Not everyone was thrilled with the Nobel committee's decision. For example, in a scathing editorial, *Life* magazine termed the prize "an extraordinary insult to America." The writer claimed, "However distinguished as a chemist, the eccentric Dr. Pauling and his weird politics have never been taken seriously by American opinion." He or she then went on to ask "Why . . . a

Pauling with his Nobel Peace Prize at his home in Big Sur, California.
(Courtesy of Pauling Archives; #325-136)

committee of five Norwegians [should] be so taken in, or so rude?"

Pauling was slighted in a number of other ways also. When he arrived in Stockholm to receive the prize, he was met by the chairman of the selection committee, but by no one from the U.S. embassy staff. The chairman commented that it was the first time in history that the ambassador of a recipient's homeland had not met the winner upon his or her arrival in Sweden.

To many people, however, Pauling's selection was entirely reasonable and justified. They were convinced that, without his constant agitation, the major powers might well have delayed even longer in agreeing to a test ban. Perhaps the supreme irony of the announcement of his winning the Peace Prize was that it came on the very day that the partial nuclear test ban treaty, signed three months earlier by the United States, the Soviet Union, and Great Britain, went into effect.

CHAPTER 8 NOTES

p. 73   "It is not necessary . . . " Tony Gray, *Champions of Peace* (New York: Paddington Press, 1976), p. 267.

p. 74   "have a destructive effect . . . " Gray, p. 267.

p. 74   "the question of peace . . . " As cited in Anthony Serafini, *Linus Pauling: A Man and His Science* (New York: Paragon House, 1989), p. 139.

p. 75   "not even a theoretical . . . " and following. Helen C. Allison, "Outspoken Scientist," *Bulletin of the Atomic Scientists*, December 1960, p. 382+.

p. 75   "I believe . . . " Linus Pauling, "My Experiences with the Internal Security Subcommittee of the United States Senate" (typed ms), September 1960, p. 7.

p. 76   "he never again. . . . " Serafini, p. 143.

p. 77   "We cannot believe . . . " As quoted in Serafini, p. 150.

p. 78   "allowing some groups . . . " As quoted in Serafini, p. 167.

p. 78   "We think it is a delusion . . . " As quoted in Gray, p. 267.

p. 79   "one of the first . . . " As quoted in Carol Pogash, "The Great Gadfly," *Science Digest*, June 1981, p. 110.

p. 80   "the audience cheered . . . " Serafini, p. 177.

p. 82   "the naive, . . . " *The New York Mirror*, June 19, 1957, as cited by Serafini, p. 183.

p. 83   "This alleged damage . . . " *Fallout and Disarmament: A Debate* (San Francisco: Fearon Publishers [n.d. 1958?]), p. 6.

p. 83   "according to . . . " *Fallout and Disarmament*, p. 8.

p. 83   "We believe . . . " *Fallout and Disarmament*, p. 12.

p. 85   "No one . . . " Pogash, p. 110.

p. 86   "provide a dramatic showdown . . . " Harry Kalven, Jr., "Congressional testing of Linus Pauling," *The Bulletin of the Atomic Scientists*, December 1960, p. 383.

p. 87   "That takes some guts . . . " Serafini, p. 211.

p. 88   "an extraordinary insult . . . " "A Weird Insult from Norway," *Life*, October 25, 1963, p. 4.

9
YEARS OF TURMOIL

For much of the 1950s, Pauling had been devoting an increasing amount of time and energy to issues unrelated to science, anti-war campaigns in general, and anti-nuclear weapons causes in particular. Yet, at no time during the decade did he totally abandon scientific research. During most of the period, the subject that especially intrigued him was molecular medicine.

The term *molecular medicine* refers to the study of diseases that can be explained on the basis of some molecular abnormality. Pauling's interest in the subject grew out of his collaboration with Harvey Itano on sickle-cell anemia. When Itano left Pasadena in 1954 to return to Washington, D.C., Pauling made up his mind to look for another disease that might have a molecular basis. He considered cancer, but decided that "almost everybody was doing research on cancer." Instead, he chose to study the less popular field of mental illness. In 1954, therefore, he requested and received from the Ford Foundation a grant to establish a research team at Cal Tech to study the molecular basis of mental disease.

The direction of this research was strongly affected by Pauling's discovery of the research of two Canadian doctors, A. Hoffer and H. Osmond, from the early 1950s. Hoffer and Osmond had found that very large doses of niacin (vitamin B_3) and ascorbic acid (vitamin C) were helpful in controlling the symptoms of schizophrenia. Pauling later explained that these results "intrigued" him. "I was fascinated by the idea that these substances, which you usually take in very small amounts . . . could have valuable health-promoting effects when ingested in amounts 100 or 1000 times greater than the usual dietary intake." He went on to tell of his search of the scientific literature, looking for further confirmation of the Hoffer and Osmond findings. What he found was that "there was a good deal of evidence to support the idea that large doses of vitamins could be clinically useful."

Pauling eventually formulated these ideas in a 1968 paper in the journal *Science* titled "Orthomolecular Psychiatry." The paper brought together ideas that had been developing over a number of years. During this time, Pauling had invented the term *orthomolecular medicines* to refer to substances that are normally present in the body, such as insulin, that can also be used for therapeutic (healing) purposes. He has explained that "Concentrations of these substances can be varied to achieve the best of health as well as disease prevention and treatment." The expression Pauling used in his 1968 paper was "the right molecules in the right amount."

In terms of treating a disorder, the principles of orthomolecular medicine mean "altering the amounts of the naturally occurring substances—vitamins, amino acids, and so on—in the human body until you find what corresponds to the concentration necessary for the best of health."

Pauling emphasizes the distinction between *orthomolecular* and *toximolecular* medicines. The latter term, he explains, refers to the more traditional medical approach, the use of toxic substances to treat disease. These toxic materials are introduced into the body to kill bacteria, viruses, or other disease-causing organisms, but they can also have harmful effects on the body itself. He compares the advantages of orthomolecular medicines that are "so free from toxicity that they show beneficial effects over a ten thousand-fold range of concentrations" in contrast to traditional drugs, such as aspirin, which can be fatal if taken in even 10 times the normal dose.

Out of Pauling's research has grown a whole new field of medicine and at least one major journal, the *Journal of Orthomolecular Psychiatry* (formed in 1971), renamed the *Journal of Orthomolecular Medicine* in 1986. Pauling's contribution to the field was acknowledged by a colleague in 1987. Dr. A. Hoffer wrote:

> *We owe an enormous debt to Linus Pauling for having made such a major contribution to medicine, for coining the word "orthomolecular," a word we can all heavily endorse, and for having given us twenty years*

of his life during which he has shown the immense importance of Vitamin C in the prevention and treatment of a variety of major diseases and minor ones including cancer and the common cold, and for fighting against a solid medical establishment unwilling to concede that he is once more correct.

Pauling's thoughts about orthomolecular medicine were influenced also by a chance event in March 1966. In his acceptance speech for receiving the Carl Newberg Medal for contributions to internal medicine, he off-handedly mentioned that he hoped to live for another 15 to 20 years to see what would be discovered in science.

About a month later, he received a letter from Irwin Stone, a biochemist who had attended the Newberg lecture. If Pauling really wanted to live a lot longer, Stone said, he should try the megavitamin therapy that he (Stone) had developed. The megavitamin therapy involved taking very large doses of vitamin C every day. People who stayed on the therapy, Stone reported, experienced an improved general sense of well-being and a greatly increased resistance to colds. (The dramatic impact of this event on Pauling's life is discussed in more detail in Chapter 10.)

Pauling demonstrated remarkable foresight in working out his concept of orthomolecular medicine. Much of the research now being done on brain chemistry follows very much the general outlines suggested by Pauling more than three decades ago.

Pauling's research interests during the 1960s were, however, by no means limited to orthomolecular medicine. Another important Pauling discovery—concerning the chemical mechanism by which anesthetics work—is an example of the process by which scientific knowledge sometimes advances. As a member of the scientific advisory board of Massachusetts General Hospital, Pauling was attending a meeting in 1952 on the use of anesthetics at the hospital. The speaker, Dr. Henry K. Beecher, described two operations in which the inert gas xenon was used as an anesthetic. Pauling was puzzled by this report. "How can xenon, which is chemically inert, be an anesthetic agent?" he asked.

Although he never conducted experiments on the question, it remained in the back of his mind for years. Then suddenly, the answer "popped into his head" one morning in April of 1959. The xenon works, he decided, because it first forms tiny crystals to which water are attached (that is, it becomes *hydrated*). These hydrated microcrystals then trap particles that transmit nerve messages in the central nervous system. The result is a loss of consciousness in the patient. Pauling spent the next two years working out the details of this theory, which he eventually published as "A Molecular Theory of General Anesthesia" in *Science* for July 7, 1961.

Pauling himself later described this event as an example of the way one's unconscious mind can take over the solution of a problem in the creative process. He explained that one technique he used in working on a problem was to think about the problem just before going to sleep.

Beyond his interest in orthomolecular medicine, Pauling appeared to have trouble finding the field of research to which he would turn next. His biographer Anthony Serafini writes that in 1963 Pauling "was not only unsure of what scientific directions he might go in, but undecided even as to which branches of knowledge he would attack next." A grant proposal that he wrote at the time for the National Science Foundation indicated that he was interested in studying the molecular basis of biological specificity, the relationship of science and civilization, the molecular basis of anesthesia, the theory of magnetism, the theory of resonance in chemical bonds, the nature of metallic bonding, the molecular basis of mental illness, aging and death, evidence for evolution from the structure of biological molecules, the structure of the atomic nucleus, and the nature of nuclear fission(!).

The range of these topic is, of course, staggering. But even more interesting is the fact that Pauling *did* pursue most of them to at least some degree in the coming years. Over the next decade, he published papers on the structure of atomic nuclei (1964), molecules as documents of evolutionary history (1965), the molecular basis of memory and consciousness (1967–69), and the characteristics of fission reactions (1969).

During the same period, Pauling also continued to write, speak, and agitate on behalf of international peace. He became particularly involved in a series of lawsuits against individuals, newspapers, and magazines that he thought had libeled him and damaged his good name.

One of the first of these suits involved the *Bellingham* (Wash.) *Herald*. During late November and early December of 1960, Pauling gave a series of addresses at ceremonies to dedicate Western Washington University's new Haggard Hall. The *Herald* published an editorial and five letters that Pauling believed reflected on his loyalty. In March 1961, Pauling sued the *Herald*'s parent company, the Bellingham Publishing Company, for the paper's remarks and for publishing the letters that he also regarded as libelous. Eventually, the paper settled out of court and paid Pauling $16,000 in damages. As part of the settlement, the *Herald* also published a retraction in its edition of May 4, 1962.

Perhaps buoyed by this success, Pauling continued to confront and to bring suits against other publications that had attacked his character. Over the next few years, some of the publications to feel his wrath were the *New York Daily News* (sued for $500,000), the *St. Louis Globe-Democrat* (for $300,000), the Hearst Publishing Company and King Features Syndicate (for $1 million), the *Syracuse Herald-Journal* and *Post-Standard*, the *Buffalo Evening News & Courier Express*, the *Newsletter of the Faculties Association, State University of New York Colleges of Education*, the *Arcadia* (Calif.) *Tribune and News*, the *Johns Hopkins Magazine*, the *Santa Barbara News-Press*, and *Nevadans on Guard*. In many cases, these publications placated Pauling by publishing a retraction or an explanatory letter by him.

Pauling's one great loss was to the magazine *National Review* and its editor, William F. Buckley, Jr. The controversy originated when the July 17, 1962, edition of the *National Review* carried a biting attack on those who sympathized with Communism in general and on Pauling in particular. Writer James Burnham criticized Pauling for "acting as a megaphone for Soviet policy" and for giving "his name, energy, voice, and pen to one after another Soviet-serving enterprise." In referring to individuals like Pauling, Burnham said that "whether they are Communists or not in the legal sense, the objective fact is that these persons . . . have given aid and comfort to the enemies of this country."

Pauling was outraged by the article and instructed his lawyer to begin legal action against the magazine. Given his track record on earlier libel suits, he probably had reason to be optimistic about the outcome of this case too.

One difference this time, however, was that Buckley refused to back down and, instead, wrote a second article even stronger than the one that had so upset Pauling. In this article, "Are You Being Sued by Linus Pauling?" Buckley wrote that Pauling seemed "to be spending his time equally between pressing for a collaborationist foreign policy and assailing those who oppose his views." Buckley warned that he and his magazine would resist the "brazen attempts at intimidation of the free press by one of the nation's leading fellow-travelers." After the article appeared, there was no longer any doubt that Pauling's suit would be heard in court.

The case dragged on until the spring of 1966 when Judge Samuel Silverman found in favor of the *National Review* and Buckley. The key element in Silverman's decision was that Pauling had become a public figure, like an elected official, and had to prove that statements about him were made with a "reckless disregard for the truth."

In fact, Buckley had argued that many of Pauling's actions in the past had actually violated the spirit or the letter of federal law. The *Review's* attacks did have, therefore, some factual basis and were not "reckless." In his final comment on the case, Buckley wrote: "There are those who believe that these conclusions [in the *Review* editorials] are in ruthless conformity with the known facts—that any other conclusion would indeed be reckless."

The political activities in which Pauling was involved after World War II increasingly had an effect on his academic affiliations. Of the roughly 85 articles he wrote in the period 1950–55, only one dealt with a political topic, the case of J. Robert Oppenheimer. In the period 1956–60, on the other hand, about 14 of 68 articles concerned political issues, and in the next five-year period, that number rose to about 46 out of 98.

Pauling's drift away from scientific research gradually became a source of some concern to his colleagues at Cal Tech. When he won the Peace Prize in 1963, he was given a reception by the biology department, but the chemistry department did nothing to honor him. Lee DuBridge, president of Cal Tech at the time, is reported to have told Pauling, "It's really a remarkable thing that someone should get a second prize, Professor Pauling; but there is of course a difference of opinion about the value of the work you have been doing." Pauling began to realize that his long, 40-year tenure at the university was becoming too strained, and he decided to leave.

Reaction to Pauling's anti-war efforts extended beyond the walls of Cal Tech. In another instance, the American Chemical Society's journal *Chemical & Engineering News* carried an article about Pauling's Nobel Peace Prize that he thought was offensive. When the journal refused to publish an apology, Pauling resigned from the organization, of which he had been a member for many years and president only a few years earlier.

An opportunity to make a break from Cal Tech presented itself in 1963 when he was offered a staff position at the Center for the Study of Democratic Institutions in Santa Barbara, California. The center had been founded in 1946 by the famous educator and former president of the University of Chicago, Robert Maynard Hutchins.

In some ways, Pauling's decision to accept this appointment is difficult to understand. The center has no facilities for scientific research and claims not to be involved in political activities. It does try to formulate a variety of positions on political issues and to educate citizens on these positions. Neither the lack of laboratory space nor the reluctance to engage in political controversy would seem to be an appealing feature to Pauling. Nonetheless, he accepted the appointment and formally resigned from his professorship at Cal Tech on June 30, 1964.

Pauling remained at Santa Barbara for four years, but his time there was not especially productive. The center was certainly a congenial place for him to pursue his peace interests, but there was little motivation for him to follow up on very many of his scientific ideas. Nonetheless, he did continue to publish about the structure of minerals, nuclear fission, the structure of atomic nuclei, chemical bond theory, and other scientific topics, while also pouring out articles and speeches on war and peace.

Eventually he decided to move on. His biographers Ted, Mildred, and Victor Goertzel report that he "felt that his role was as a theorist, elder statesman, and scientific gadfly, and he sought a situation where younger men would carry out his research ideas." So, in 1967 he accepted an appointment to the chemistry faculty at the University of California at San Diego (UCSD).

UCSD seemed a more appropriate setting for Pauling's scientific interests. For one thing, there was a ready supply of graduate students in chemistry, available to carry out Pauling's research ideas. Probably more important, however, was the opportunity for Pauling to renew a friendship with a former Cal Tech student of his, Arthur Robinson. Robinson had gone on to become a professor of chemistry himself and was then employed at UCSD. Robinson shared some of Pauling's ideas about and interest in orthomolecular medicine and agreed to take charge of Pauling's laboratory at UCSD.

Pauling and Robinson collaborated on a number of studies and wrote 11 papers together between 1970 and 1975. Although most of those papers dealt with orthomolecular medicine, others had to do with totally unrelated subjects such as the structure of atomic nuclei. Pauling's association with Robinson was to grow stronger and stronger for a decade. At one point, Pauling apparently referred to Robinson as "my principal and most valued collaborator." Then, in 1978, the relationship suddenly collapsed with bitterness and recriminations (see Chapter 10).

In any case, Pauling's association with UCSD lasted only two years. Whether he left San Diego because he was bored, as one group of biographers claim, or because he felt he had been slighted by the university administration, as another biographer believes, he resigned his position there in 1969.

His next move was just up the coast to Stanford University. In a statement to the press, Pauling offered yet another reason for his move from UCSD to Stanford. The state university system was beginning to feel severe financial pressures as a result of Governor Ronald Reagan's austerity measures. Among the factors that convinced Pauling to leave UCSD, he said, was "the present uncertainty about continued financial support of the University of California." He also criticized the governor's efforts to take decision-making authority out of the hands of faculties and give it to the Board of Regents. Finally, Pauling expressed some unhappiness with the pressures brought on him at UCSD by conservative citizens of San Diego.

When Pauling left UCSD for Stanford, Robinson found himself in a difficult situation. His career had become closely mingled with Pauling's. It is hardly surprising, given their ongoing collaboration and mutual respect, that Pauling was able to convince Robinson to join him part-time at Stanford. Since Robinson still held a full-time appointment at UCSD, the Stanford work with Pauling could only be done on weekends, during vacations, or while on academic leave from his regular job. The early 1970s were not an easy time for Arthur Robinson!

Pauling was to remain at Stanford until 1974 when he reached mandatory retirement age. Stanford then awarded him the honorary position of emeritus professor. He was by no means ready to retire, however. Instead, he struck out with Robinson and another

Original home of the Pauling Institute at Menlo Park, California. (Courtesy of Linus Pauling Institute of Science and Medicine/Menlo Park)

Current home of the Pauling Institute in Palo Alto, California. (Courtesy of Linus Pauling Institute of Science and Medicine/Palo Alto)

colleague, Keene Dimick, to establish a new institution, the Institute of Orthomolecular Medicine, eventually to be renamed the Linus Pauling Institute of Science and Medicine, in Palo Alto, California.

Finding financial resources to get the institute operating was difficult, and most of the original money came from Pauling and Robinson themselves. The doors finally opened in 1975, however, with Pauling as tenured faculty member for life and Robinson tenured until age 65. It seemed that Pauling at last had the institution where he could work exactly as he liked: his *own* institution! The future looked bright indeed, and there was little hint of the internal dissensions that would soon nearly tear the new institution apart.

CHAPTER 9 NOTES

p. 92   "almost everybody . . . " "The Plowboy Interview: Dr. Linus Pauling," *Mother Earth News*, January/February 1978, p. 18.

p. 92　　"I was fascinated . . . " and following quotation. "The Plowboy Interview," p. 18.

p. 93　　"Concentrations . . . " Neil A. Campbell, "Crossing the Boundaries of Science," *BioScience*, December 1986, p. 738.

p. 93　　"altering the amounts . . . " "The Plowboy Interview," p. 18.

p. 93　　"so free from . . . " Campbell, p. 738.

p. 93　　"We owe . . . " A. Hoffer, review of *The Roots of Molecular Medicine—A Tribute to Linus Pauling*, Richard P. Huewer, ed., in *Journal of Orthomolecular Medicine*, Third Quarter 1987, pp. 196–197.

p. 94　　"How can xenon . . . " Campbell, p. 739.

p. 95　　"was not only unsure . . . " Anthony Serafini, *Linus Pauling: A Man and His Science* (New York: Paragon House, 1989), p. 222.

p. 96　　"acting as a megaphone . . . " "The Collaborators," *National Review*, July 17, 1962, p. 9. Also see James Burnham, "Treason a la mode," *National Review*, December 31, 1960, p. 403.

p. 97　　"to be spending . . . " "Are You Being Sued by Linus Pauling?" *National Review*, September 25, 1962, p. 218.

p. 97　　"There are those . . . " "*National Review* Vindicated," May 3, 1966, p. 404.

p. 98　　"It's really . . . " As quoted in Serafini, p. 218.

p. 99　　"felt that . . . " Ted G. Goertzel, Mildred George Goertzel, and Victor Goertzel, "Linus Pauling: The Scientist as Crusader," *Antioch Review*, Summer 1980, p. 377.

p. 99　　"my principal . . . " as quoted in Arthur B. Robinson, "Letter to the Editor," *Antioch Review*, Summer 1981, p. 383.

p. 99　　"the present uncertainty . . . " "Stanford Lures Pauling," *Industrial Research*, June 1969, p. 38.

10

LINUS PAULING AND VITAMIN C

An alien transported to Earth after 1970 might reasonably believe that the name *Linus Pauling* is associated with only one subject: vitamin C. During that period of time, Pauling devoted a majority of his time and energy to thinking, writing, and speaking about vitamin C, first as a way of protecting against the common cold, and later as a possible therapy for cancer. His book *Vitamin C and the Common Cold*, written in 1970, has been followed by more than 125 articles and letters in a half dozen languages on the benefits of vitamin C therapy.

Irwin Stone's 1966 letter to Pauling about megavitamin theory did not appear to mark a turning point in Pauling's life at the time. He and Ava Helen decided to give Stone's ideas a try and began to notice "an increased feeling of well-being . . . and we discovered that we no longer caught colds."

But that discovery did not lead Pauling to begin campaigning for the virtues of vitamin C (also known as ascorbic acid). It was not until three years later that that transformation occurred. The occasion was a short speech that Pauling delivered at the Mount Sinai Medical School in which he briefly alluded to the value of vitamin C in preventing colds.

A short time later, Pauling received a strongly worded letter from a professor, Victor Herbert, who had attended the lecture. "Do you want to support the vitamin quacks that are bleeding the American public of millions of dollars a year?" he asked. He challenged Pauling to show him "a single double-blind study that indicates that vitamin C has any more value than a placebo in fighting colds."

(A double-blind study is one in which neither researchers nor subjects know which individuals are getting the treatment and which are getting a harmless, inactive material, the *placebo.*)

Pauling's immediate response was that he did *not* know of any such studies. But he decided to find out if any existed. Eventually he located a number of studies that supported the concept of megavitamin therapy, and he sent one of the most promising, by a scientist named Ritzel, to Herbert. Herbert's response to Pauling was "I am not impressed by the work of Ritzel," although he failed to say *why* he was not impressed. Pauling wrote back to Herbert, "I'm not impressed by your saying that *you're* not impressed by the work of Ritzel."

The result of this whole exchange with Herbert was that Pauling "became sufficiently irritated by this fellow" that he decided to mount an all-out attack on the question of vitamin C therapy. He read everything he could find on the subject and by July of 1970 was ready to start writing his book on the subject, *Vitamin C and the Common Cold.* He finished the manuscript in two months and the book was published on November 17 of the same year. The book has since been reprinted a number of times and has been translated into Danish, Dutch, French, German, Hindi, Japanese, Norwegian, Portuguese, and Swedish.

Medical scientists had mixed reactions to Pauling's book. Some agreed that megavitamin theory for treatment of the common cold was at least a reasonable idea that deserved to be tested. Others thought, however, that Pauling had "gone off the deep end" and was spouting nonsense about a topic that he was not qualified to write about.

One who was impressed by Pauling's book was a British nutritionist, Reginald Passmore, who called the book "first-class popular scientific writing." Among Pauling's critics, however, was Frederick J. Stare of the Harvard School of Public Health. Stare claimed that Pauling had no training in nutrition and was "lost in the woods" with the vitamin C theory.

One of the problems with Pauling's position was that the evidence from research on megavitamin therapy was not very clear. For every study that appeared to support or oppose the theory, critics could find something to argue about. The correct dose of vitamin C had not been used, subjects were not properly selected, inappropriate measurements were taken, researchers misinterpreted their own findings, and so on. Even today, more than 20 years after Pauling began his studies of vitamin C, scientists cannot agree as to what effect, if any, the compound has on the common cold.

As time went on, however, Pauling became more and more convinced about the value of megavitamin therapy. He eventually came to the conclusion that all humans are chronically in a condition of hypoascorbemia, that is, vitamin C deficiency. Compared to other animals who take in up to five grams of vitamin C in their normal diets, humans expect to get along with no more than 45 milligrams of the vitamin. While medical researchers believe that this is enough to maintain "ordinary good health," it actually causes humans to be, Pauling believes, in a state of "ordinary poor health."

If it were possible to dramatically increase the level of vitamin C in our diets, Pauling has said, we would dramatically increase our resistance to all of the infectious diseases, including measles, mumps, pneumonia, meningitis, chicken pox, hepatitis, and influenza. He has recently written also about the potential value of vitamin C in treating HIV infection. The reason for the vitamin's success in dealing with the wide range of disease, Pauling has argued, is its ability to potentiate (activate) the immune system. By some as-yet-unknown mechanism, he believes, vitamin C helps natural immune reactions to combat infectious agents more efficiently.

Pauling's studies of megavitamin therapy took a significant turn in 1971 when he learned of studies in Scotland in which large doses of vitamin C were used to treat cancer patients. In those studies, carried out by Dr. Ewan Cameron, cancer patients were given up to 10 grams of vitamin C each day. Cameron reported that the most seriously ill patients experienced improvements that ranged from decreased pain to temporary remission to apparently permanent cure of the disease.

These results were, of course, very exciting to Pauling. They supported his view that vitamin C may be useful, not only in treating relatively mild conditions like the common cold, but also far more serious diseases such as cancer. In a public lecture at the

University of Chicago he predicted that "with the proper uses of ascorbic acid the mortality from cancer could be reduced by about ten percent." On another occasion he went even further. He wrote in 1977 that

> *In 1971, I published my opinion that a decrease of 10 percent in the age-specific incidence of and mortality from cancer could be achieved by use of vitamin C. There is far more information now than was available in 1971, and my present estimate is that a decrease of 75 percent can be achieved by use of vitamin C alone, and a further decrease by use of other nutritional measures.*

A number of medical scientists thought that Pauling was exaggerating the effects of vitamin C. They were not convinced that existing evidence supported such strong statements as a "ten percent" or "75 percent" rate of cure. Pauling began to experience significant and sometimes hostile opposition from fellow scientists. Perhaps the most important of these was the May 1972 decision by the editorial board of the *Proceedings of the National Academy of Sciences* not to publish Pauling's paper on cancer and vitamin C. The decision was especially remarkable since members of the National Academy of Sciences (as Pauling was) have historically had essentially free access to the *Proceedings* as an outlet for their work. That policy had been established in 1914 and had, until the 1972 decision, never been violated.

Pauling was, understandably, furious. He insisted that the editorial board had no right to prevent publication of a member's papers. The board's action amounted to censorship, he said, and "This sort of censorship is pretty dangerous."

The opposition he was experiencing did not deter Pauling from pursuing his theory further. In 1975, he initiated a second study with Ewan Cameron of the latter's patients at Vale of Leven Hospital in Scotland. This study was very carefully designed with exact matches between control (those not receiving the treatment) and experimental subjects. The study was especially important since it was an actual experiment in comparison with Cameron's original research, which involved no more than the study of patient records.

The result of this experiment, accepted this time by the *Proceedings of the National Academy of Sciences*, showed that patients who received vitamin C lived, on the average, 4.2 times as long as the control patients. Pauling was enthusiastic about these results and suggested that they might have been even more pronounced if patients had started taking vitamin C earlier and taken larger doses of it.

In the midst of these apparently hopeful results from Scotland, Pauling received disappointing news from another research institution: his own Linus Pauling Institute of Science and Medicine. Arthur Robinson was conducting a very large, carefully planned study of cancer in mice that were fed: (1) only raw fruits and vegetables, or (2) regular diets combined with large doses of vitamin C, or (3) raw fruits and vegetables combined with large doses of vitamin C.

Robinson's research produced apparently conflicting results. On one hand, mice that were fed a normal diet and vitamin C developed more cancers than those who got no vitamin C at all. On the other hand, mice that were given raw fruits and vegetables *and* vitamin C got the fewest cancers of any group in the study. The data could be used to argue that vitamin C prevents cancer or causes cancer. Obviously, additional studies needed to be done.

Pauling's view seemed to be, however, that Robinson's results were potentially damaging to the vitamin C–cancer theory and that it would be inappropriate for his own institute to publish data contradicting a concept in which he so totally believed. As a result, he ordered Robinson to turn his records over to him and to leave the institute for at least a year. When Robinson refused to do so, Pauling became "livid," according to a group of his biographers, and he "threatened to have the mice killed in order to prevent continuation of the experiment."

The dispute rapidly became more ugly. Trustees of the institute withheld Robinson's salary, suspended him from his job, and locked up his files. In response, Robinson filed a series of law suits against the institute, its trustees, and Pauling totaling more than $25 million. After years of litigation, those suits were finally settled out of court in 1983. Robinson was, however, forced to leave the institute where he had once held a position that gave him tenure to the age of 65.

After leaving Palo Alto, Robinson moved to the Oregon Institute of Science and Medicine where he continued his research on vitamin C and cancer. That research produced additional results that seemed to confirm his earlier work at Palo Alto. Eventually he wrote Pauling suggesting that a "public warning should be issued" concerning the possible dangers of ingesting large amounts of vitamin C. Pauling never replied to this letter.

Pauling's own views on vitamin C and cancer were obviously not affected by Robinson's research or his conclusions on the topic. In 1981, Pauling finally obtained a grant from the National Cancer Institute (NCI) to study the effects of vitamin C on breast cancer in mice. The grant came after four previous applications going back to 1973 had not been funded. Pauling received the award at least partly because he lobbied legislators and administration officials so aggressively. As one NCI official explained, Pauling's activities were "meant to badger us." Staff at NCI eventually "lent a special hand" to see that Pauling got his award.

A possible definitive answer to the vitamin C–cancer question appeared to be on the horizon in 1978. The prestigious Mayo Clinic in Rochester, Minnesota, decided to do a thorough study of the issue. The results they reported in late 1979 failed to show any therapeutic effect of the vitamin. The Mayo researchers suggested that the case was closed for vitamin C.

It took Pauling relatively little time to find a fundamental flaw in the Mayo study. Researchers had included in the study patients who had earlier received large doses of chemotherapy. Such patients would have had severely damaged immune systems, Pauling pointed out, and would not have been able to benefit from vitamin C therapy. In fact, Pauling had warned Mayo researchers in advance of this effect.

Pauling's objections apparently had some effect, for Mayo designed a second study on vitamin C and cancer, one that supposedly avoided the methodological problems associated with the first study. Once again, researchers found no positive effects from the use of vitamin C. The case was *really* closed this time, the Mayo researchers believed. The report of the second study concluded, "It is very clear that this study fails to show a benefit for high-dose vitamin C therapy of advanced cancer."

As might be expected, Pauling was still not satisfied with the results and found yet new problems with the study's methodology. He pointed out, for example, that none of the Mayo patients died while they were taking vitamin C, although they did after the vitamin therapy was concluded. The study, he suggested, had simply ended too soon.

In fact, the question about vitamin C and cancer is probably still not resolved to everyone's satisfaction. Pauling's biographer Anthony Serafini concludes, even after the carefully planned Mayo studies, "The objective truth about vitamin C has yet to be revealed. . . . More work is needed."

Throughout the vitamin C controversies, Pauling continued to receive awards and honors. Among these were the International Lenin Peace Prize (1971), the Lomonosov Gold Medal of the Soviet Academy of Sciences (1978), the Priestley Medal of the American Chemical Society (1984), the American Chemical Society Award in Chemical Education (1987), and the Vannevar Bush Award of the National Science Foundation (1989).

In some ways, the most satisfying award may have been the National Medal of Science, presented to Pauling by President Gerald Ford on September 18, 1975. Pauling's strong objections to the Vietnam War, which he had called "as obscene as anything could be," had made him as unwelcome in the Nixon White House as it had to the Eisenhower administration in the 1950s. Even his position as a double Nobel laureate had not been sufficient to overcome Nixon's suspicions and dislike of him.

Ford's decision to honor Pauling in 1975 was part of the President's efforts to bring healing to the nation after the fiasco of the Nixon Watergate years. Science advisor H. Guyford Stever explained that "the award is part of a mood of conciliation throughout our nation. . . . We disagree on politics pretty strongly at times, but science is science, and what Pauling has done in science has been of importance to all the people of the world."

Pauling also continued to write, of course. Between his 80th and 90th birthdays, he produced 180 more articles, letters, reviews, and other publications. In addition to familiar topics such as crystal structure, megavitamin therapy, and world peace, Pauling also wrote about the potential health effects of electromagnetic radiation, one of the first important scientists to recognize this potential health issue.

Most prominent among these works was yet another book, *How to Live Longer and Feel Better*, published in 1986. The book attempts to show how principles of orthomolecular medicine and megavitamin nutrition can be used to attain better health and longer life. Pauling's promotion of the book was so aggressive that the great science writer Isaac Asimov worried that a younger generation might not fully realize the significance of Pauling's "lesser-known, more serious work."

Even his 90th birthday did not bring any slowdown in his research or writing. He announced in 1992 that his next book would deal with yet another aspect of his megavitamin theory, the relationship between vitamin C and heart disease.

Tragedy struck Pauling in 1981 when his beloved wife of 58 years died of stomach cancer. Ava Helen Pauling had been diagnosed with the disease in 1975, but she scarcely slowed down after receiving the news. She continued to write and speak about causes

Linus and Ava Helen at home, about 1960. (Courtesy of Pauling Archives; #324-131)

that were important to her and to be at her husband's side during his battles and honors. In a 1977 interview she explained that since he would never retire, she couldn't either. "I'd feel guilty," she said.

In looking back over her life, she reflected that much of her life had been devoted to her husband and her children. Still, she had managed to dedicate a considerable amount of time and energy to causes that were important to her. In recognition of those efforts, San Gabriel College awarded her an honorary doctorate which, she said, she thought she deserved. It was for her social and political work. "I took the lead in our peace efforts," she explained. "I was active in the ACLU, against the war and against putting Japanese-Americans in camps." At least as important, her husband pointed out, was her influence in recruiting Pauling to the peace movement.

The Paulings' children all became successful in their own fields, a not-insignificant accomplishment when growing up with a father as famous and as controversial as Linus Pauling. Linus, Jr., became a psychiatrist and led the Hawaii delegation in the Selma, Alabama, civil rights march. The Paulings related that they were "a little surprised and very pleased" at this act because, as Ava Helen said, Linus, Jr., is an M.D. and "they tend to be very conservative."

Peter remained in London after his graduate work there, eventually becoming a lecturer in chemistry at University College at the University of London. In 1975, he coauthored a general chemistry textbook with his father. Crellin, the Paulings' youngest son, became professor of genetics at the University of California at Riverside, and their daughter, Linda, is married to a professor at Cal Tech.

Linus Pauling was confronted with yet one more challenge in 1991. His doctors informed him in December that he had cancer of the prostate. Six months later, however, he reported that he was fully recovered from the disease. A conventional treatment of the drug glutamine supplemented, of course, by vitamin C, appeared to have been successful. "I never contended that you can control a disease completely forever," he said, "but improved nutrition can shift the mortality curve." It was obvious that Pauling was going to be around at least a bit longer to fight the battles that were important to him.

CHAPTER 10 NOTES

p. 103   "an increased feeling . . . " "The Plowboy Interview: Dr. Linus Pauling," *Mother Earth News*, January/February 1978, p. 18.

p. 103   "Do you want . . . " "The Plowboy Interview," p. 18.

p. 104   "first-class . . . " Rae Goodell, *The Visible Scientists* (New York: Paddington Press, 1976), pp. 82-83.

p. 105   "ordinary poor health . . . " "The Plowboy Interview," p. 20.

p. 106   "with the proper uses . . . Anthony Serafini, *Linus Pauling: A Man and His Science* (New York: Paragon House, 1989), p. 245.

p. 106   "In 1971 . . . " "Vitamin C Research Roadblocked," *Prevention*, November 1977, p. 173.

p. 106   "This sort . . . " Barbara J. Culliton, "Academy Turns Down a Pauling Paper," *Science*, August 4, 1972, p. 409.

p. 107   "threatened to have . . . " Ted G. Goertzel, Mildred George Goertzel, and Victor Goertzel, "Linus Pauling: The Scientist as Crusader," *Antioch Review*, Summer 1980, p. 379.

p. 108   "meant to badger . . . " Marjorie Sun, "At Long Last, Linus Pauling Lands NCI Grant," *Science*, June 5, 1981, p. 1126.

p. 108   "It is very clear . . . " Charles G. Moertel, et al., "High-dose Vitamin C versus Placebo in the Treatment of Patients with Advanced Cancer Who Have Had No Prior Chemotherapy," *New England Journal of Medicine*, January 17, 1985, p. 141.

p. 109   "The objective truth . . " Serafini, p. 283.

p. 109   "as obscene . . . " William F. Fry, Jr., "What's New with You, Linus Pauling?" *The Humanist*, November/December 1974, p. 18.

p. 109   "the award . . . " Luther J. Carter, "Pauling Gets Medal of Science: Thaw Between Scientists and White House," *Science*, October 3, 1975, p. 33.

p. 110   "lesser-known . . . " Serafini, p. xx.

p. 111   "I took the lead . . . " Mildred Hamilton, "The Unretir-
           ing Paulings," *San Francisco Examiner & Chronicle*,
           August 21, 1977, p. 2 Scene.
p. 111   "a little surprised . . . " "The Unretiring Paulings," p. 2
           Scene.
p. 111   "I never contended . . . " Marvine Howe, "Chronicle,"
           New York Times, May 15, 1992, p. 4.

11

LINUS PAULING: THE MAN AND THE LEGACY

The personal lives of geniuses are at least as complex as those of ordinary mortals. Intellectual brilliance, after all, does not necessarily guarantee moral integrity, personal charm, political rectitude, or any other desirable character trait. So one should hardly be surprised that Linus Pauling's life and personality have been assessed in a myriad of ways by his contemporaries.

The one point on which no one disagrees is his brilliance as a scientist. Probably the most prolific and one of the best-known science writers of all time, Isaac Asimov, has called him "a first-class genius," "the greatest chemist of the twentieth century." Pauling's numerous honorary degrees and awards confirm this judgment. His colleagues have honored him at one time or another with every high honor in chemistry.

Of special significance has been Pauling's willingness to remain active in chemical research late in life. Some Nobel Prize winners are little known after making the one great discovery for which they are honored. James Watson, co-discoverer of the structure of DNA, is an example. After receiving his Nobel Prize in 1962, Watson became more interested in the administration of science and essentially abandoned scientific research. In contrast, Pauling has continued to write on topics such as nuclear structure, resonance, crystal structure, and quasi-crystals into his 90th year.

But what of Linus Pauling the man? Much less agreement exists on this point. To his admirers, Pauling is not only a genius, but a man of the highest character. Asimov continues his praise of

Pauling in his office at his home in Big Sur, California, 1987. (Courtesy of Pauling Archives; #325-131)

Pauling by calling him "a gentleman in the highest sense of the word. He has *character.*"

Many who know Pauling would agree with Asimov's assessment. His biographers Ted, Mildred, and Victor Goertzel write about his "radiant smile, brilliant wit, and vigorous enthusiasm for his work [that] give him great charismatic appeal." His efforts on behalf of peace have been especially noted. Numerous supporters have praised him for his "independence, courage, and fighting qualities," and called him "an outstanding example of the kind of scientist who is more needed now . . . one chiefly concerned with the humanely useful applications of scientific knowledge." In one article, he is described as "a stubborn idealist [who] still wears his well-developed sense of morality, like his jaunty black beret, wherever he travels."

The same article allows Pauling to describe his own ethical code:

> *The evidence of my senses tells me that I am a man like other men. When I cut myself, I am hurt, I suffer. I cry out. I see that when someone else cuts himself, he cries out. I conclude from his behavior that he is suffering in the same way that I was . . . I am led to believe that I am a man like other men.*
>
> *I want to be free of suffering to the greatest extent possible. I should like to live a happy, useful life, a satisfying life. I want other people to help keep my suffering to a minimum. It is my duty, accordingly, to help them, to strive to prevent suffering for other people.*

Yet, there is another side to Linus Pauling's character. The Goertzels conclude: "Pauling is a classic example of a person who loves humanity but doesn't care much for people. He is generally without close friends. . . . Politically, he is a crusader for his vision of truth with little tolerance for considering the viewpoints of others."

Indeed, one cannot understand Linus Pauling the man without appreciating his own enormous self-confidence. A colleague has observed that he is "very rarely wrong about anything. For him to be modest would be hypocrisy." It is hardly surprising, then, to read so often about Pauling in terms of his "enormous ego," his "bracing self-regard," or his "mind of his own."

Nor is it surprising, therefore, to hear about the almost constant battles with individuals and organizations that have characterized

Pauling's life. Perhaps the most remarkable feature of Anthony Serafini's biography of Pauling is the recurring theme of his personal disputes with professional colleagues and political figures. Serafini devotes the better part of five chapters to the most famous of these disputes with British mathematician and biologist Dorothy Wrinch, Nobel Prize winning biologist Herman J. Müller, political columnist William F. Buckley, Jr., and former student and cofounder of the Linus Pauling Institute, Arthur Robinson.

The last of these disputes illustrates how bitter these controversies sometimes became. After his initial reluctance to talk about his disagreement with Robinson, Pauling eventually began to make his case in speeches, articles, and letters to editors. In a 1981 letter to the *Antioch Review*, Pauling called the Goertzels' article about his feud with Robinson "astonishingly incorrect and misleading."

In turn, Robinson offered his own three-page review of the controversy in the following issue of the *Antioch Review*. In his own letter, Robinson accuses Pauling of never organizing, directing, or carrying out any research at the institute that bears his name. He points out that "Linus has not personally contributed significant research work on vitamin C and human health, although he has been politically successful in obtaining credit for Ewan Cameron's work in Scotland." His letter criticizes Pauling for making false claims, for his "rage" and "virulent outbreaks" at Robinson personally, and for the "ruthlessness" with which he conducted some of his scientific research.

The bitterness of Robinson's letter helps explain the Goertzels' own final thoughts on Pauling's life, namely that "we have been forced to reconsider our assumption that a great humanitarian must necessarily be an outstanding human being . . . The same egocentricity that makes a man a tyrant in a position of power may also produce an effective resister of the oppression and orthodoxies of others."

So how will Linus Pauling be remembered by historians a hundred years from now? In some ways, Pauling's most fundamental claim to fame is based on the fact that he almost single-handedly reshaped the way practitioners looked at their field, He showed how mathematical and physical methods, especially quantum mechanics, could be brought to bear on topics to which they had never been applied so thoroughly before.

He eventually went one step further and showed how mathematics, physics, and chemistry can all be integrated in the study of the molecules of which all living organisms are composed and how that study can provide an entirely new insight on the structure and function of living beings.

Without much question, Pauling's most significant specific accomplishment has probably been his work on the nature of the chemical bond. He began that work at a time when the term *chemical bond* had essentially little concrete meaning. Lewis and Langmuir had just begun to outline the way in which the attraction between two atoms could be described in terms of electronic configuration. More than any other single individual, Pauling was ultimately to refine that concept and express it in a form that is essentially that used by chemists today.

Another important achievement has been Pauling's emphasis on the significance of molecular architecture in understanding the nature of matter. His earliest research at Cal Tech revealed the structure of hundreds of minerals. But the extension of that research to biological molecules has been even more significant. Scientists have gradually come to understand that the biological functions that molecules have is largely dependent on their physical shape. That understanding, in turn, has become possible largely through the line of research pioneered by Pauling. In this regard, he must be considered one of the founders of the modern science of molecular biology.

Pauling's early concepts of orthomolecular medicine also appear to have been at least partially confirmed in recent years. Scientists now have a much better understanding of the way specific chemicals behave in the body, especially in the brain. Pauling's notion that some mental disorders may result from a deficiency of naturally occurring compounds appears to be correct and may well form the basis for more productive research in the future.

Pauling's research in other areas is perhaps less well known, but valuable in its own way. During the mid-1960s, he "dabbled" in the topic of nuclear physics and eventually developed a theory about nuclear structure. It never had much impact, for a variety of reasons, but one colleague thought that "had it been done some forty years earlier . . . physicists might have found it quite useful."

Pauling's accomplishments outside the field of science are more debatable. The Nobel Peace Prize confirms the view of some that his campaigns against nuclear weapons testing in particular and against war in general had an important impact on the course of human history in the 1950s and 1960s.

His critics disagree. They argue that the fact that Pauling was outspoken does not mean that he was influential. They suggest that other factors, such as the Cuban missile crisis of 1962, may have been even more responsible for the nuclear test ban treaty that the United States and the Soviet Union eventually signed.

Nor is it clear where Pauling's advocacy of megavitamin therapy is to lead. Most authorities seem to believe that the scientific evidence for Pauling's theories is still not available and may never be. However, enough questions appear to remain to justify further research on Pauling's current field of special interest.

Pauling will be remembered also, not for his specific contributions to knowledge, but for his approach to problem-solving. We are often taught that the road to scientific knowledge consists of many individual bricks, specific bits of information collected painstakingly one piece at a time. Only when these many units of knowledge have been collected, we are told, can someone assemble them into some grand theory.

And that system does work. But Pauling has reminded us of another approach. At times, one may see the answer first, and then go back to look for the evidence needed to support the answer. In working on molecular structures, for example, he often constructed a model early on in his research, then used data to test the model. It was this approach that led Pauling to his discovery of the helical structure of the protein molecule and, ironically, to the discovery of the DNA structure by two competitors, Crick and Watson.

It seems certain that Pauling, like a handful of the greatest scientists, will always be remembered not for a single discovery but as a brilliant, complex, controversial figure. For all his flaws and weaknesses, an individual like Linus Pauling does not come along often enough in human history.

CHAPTER 11 NOTES

p. 114   "a first-class . . . " Anthony Serafini, *Linus Pauling: A Man and His Science* (New York: Paragon House, 1989), pp. xii and xvi.

p. 116   "a gentleman . . . " Serafini, p. xvi.

p. 116   "radiant smile . . . " Ted G. Goertzel, Mildred George Goertzel, and Victor Goertzel, "Linus Pauling: The Scientist as Crusader," *Antioch Review*, Summer 1980, p. 382.

p. 116   "independence, courage, . . . " Helen C. Allison, "Outspoken Scientist," *Bulletin of the Atomic Scientists*, December 1960, p. 390; and "an outstanding example . . . " Dorris Planz, "The Vitamin C Controversy," *The Nation*, April 5, 1971, p. 441.

p. 116   "a stubborn idealist . . . " Carol Pogash, "The Great Gadfly," *Science Digest*, June 1981, p. 90.

p. 116   "Pauling is . . . " "Linus Pauling: The Scientist as Crusader," p. 382.

p. 116   "very rarely wrong . . . " "The Great Gadfly," p. 90.

p. 116   "bracing self-regard," George W. Gray, "Pauling and Beadle," *Scientific American*, May 1949, p. 16; "mind of his own," Marjorie Sun, "At Long Last, Linus Pauling Lands NCI Grant," *Science*, June 5, 1981, p. 1127.

p. 117   "Linus has not . . . " Arthur B. Robinson, "Letter to the Editor," *Antioch Review*, Summer 1981, p. 384.

p. 117   "we have been forced . . . " "Linus Pauling: The Scientist as Crusader," p. 382.

p. 119   "had it been done . . . " As quoted in Serafini, p. 226.

GLOSSARY

amino acid: an organic compound whose characteristic functional groups are an amino group ($-NH_2$) and a carboxyl group (-COOH); the basic unit of which all proteins are made.

antibody: a protein produced by the body as a defensive response to the presence of some foreign material in the body, an *antigen.*

antigen: any foreign substance that appears in an organism's body and initiates an antibody response from that organism.

atom: the smallest particle of an element that displays all the characteristics of that element.

azimuthal quantum number: A quantum number indicating the degree of ellipticity of an electron's orbit around an atomic nucleus.

compound: a substance that consists of two or more elements combined with each other chemically in some constant proportion.

covalent bond: a force of attraction that exists between two atoms as a result of their sharing a pair of electrons between them.

electron: one of the fundamental particles of matter, a lepton, whose mass is approximately 0.511 MeV and whose electrical charges is -1.

electronegativity: the relative tendency of an atom to attract to itself the electrons in a bond that it shares with some other atom.

element: a substance that cannot be broken down into any simpler material by ordinary chemical means.

enzyme: a protein or protein-containing substance that catalyzes a biochemical reaction.

hybridization: the tendency of two or more atomic orbitals to combine with each other to form a new orbital.

ionic bond: a force of attraction that exists between two ions with opposite electrical charges.

molecule: two or more atoms held together by some chemical force. A molecule is the smallest particle of an element or compound that displays all the characteristics of that element or compound.

orbital: an energy state of an electron determined by its specific location in an atom. Any one eletronic orbital has unique values of quantum numbers n, 1, and m.

peptide: a term used to describe the combination of amino acids. For example, the bond joining two amino acids is called a *peptide bond*, and the combination of three peptides is referred to as a *tripeptide*.

photoelectric effect: the release of electrons from a material as a result of its being exposed to electromagnetic radiation.

protein: a very large molecule consisting of very long chains of amino acids joined to each other.

quantum: (plural: *quanta*) the smallest unit of energy that can exist.

quantum number: one of a set of numbers that describes the energy state of an electron or some other particle.

quantum theory: the modern theory of matter and electromagnetic energy that states that the transfer of energy can occur only in discrete units called quanta.

resonance: a concept used to describe some composite or average structure of two or more possible structures.

substrate: any substance that is acted upon by an enzyme.

wavelength: the distance between two crests or two troughs of a wave.

X-ray crystallography: a technique for determining the structure of a crystalline material by directing a beam of X rays at a sample of that substance.

X-ray diffraction photograph: the pattern produced on a photographic plate as the result of shining X rays on a crystal of some material.

FURTHER READING

Linus Pauling has written an enormous number of books, articles, letters to editors, and other works. The majority of these are highly technical in character and will be of interest only to the reader with a strong background in chemistry. However, a number of Pauling's works are easily accessible to the reader with no background in science at all. His books and articles on peace and vitamin C are examples. A few items that are particularly recommended are the following:

Cameron, Ewan, and Linus Pauling. *Cancer and Vitamin C*. Palo Alto, CA: Linus Pauling Institute of Science and Medicine, 1979.

"Linus Pauling Talks about Soviet Testing." *U.S. News & World Report*, October 2, 1961, 94–95.

Pauling, Linus, "Chemistry and the World of Tomorrow." *Chemical & Engineering News*, April 16, 1984, 54–56.

———. "Early Days of Molecular Biology in the California Institute of Technology." *Annual Review of Biophysical Chemistry*, 1986, 1–9.

———. "Fifty Years of Physical Chemistry in the California Institute of Technology." In *Annual Review of Physical Chemistry*, vol. 16, H. Eyring, ed., Palo Alto, CA: Annual Reviews, Inc., 1965.

———. "Fifty Years of Progress in Structural Chemistry and Molecular Biology" *Daedalus*, Fall 1970, 988–1014.

———. *How to Live Longer and Feel Better*. New York: W. H. Freeman, 1986.

———. "Orthomolecular Psychiatry: Varying the Concentrations of Substances Normally Present in the Human Body May Control Mental Disease." *Science*, April 19, 1968, 265–271.

———. "Pauling on G. N. Lewis." *Chemtech*, June 1983, 334–337.

———. "The Social Responsibilities of Scientists and Science." *The Science Teacher*, May 1966, 14–18.

———. *Vitamin C and the Common Cold*. San Francisco: W. H. Freeman, 1970.

————.*Vitamin C, the Common Cold, and the Flu*. San Francisco: W. H. Freeman, 1976.

————."What Can We Expect for Chemistry in the Next 100 Years?" *Chemical & Engineering News*, April 19, 1976, 33–36.

————."Why Modern Chemistry Is Quantum Chemistry." *New Scientist*, November 7, 1985, 54–55.

The definitive biography of Pauling thus far is the one written by Anthony Serafini. Although the chronology is sometimes difficult to follow, the book is a treasure mine of information about Pauling's life. A second biography, by Florence Meiman White, is designed for younger readers. It has some interesting information on Pauling's early life and personal experiences later in life. Interested readers should also be aware of a new biography on Pauling by Tom Hager, scheduled for publication by Simon & Schuster in 1994.

Serafini, Anthony. *Linus Pauling: A Man and His Science*. New York: Paragon House, 1989.

White, Florence Meiman. *Linus Pauling: Scientist and Crusader* New York: Walker & Co., 1980.

Pauling's life and work are also discussed in detail in a number of anthologies, most important of which are:

Goodell, Rae. *The Visible Scientists*. Boston: Little, Brown, 1977.

Gray, Tony. *Champions of Peace*. New York: Paddington Press, 1976.

"Linus Pauling." *Current Biography 1964*. New York: H. W. Wilson, 1964, 339–342.

"Linus Pauling." *Current Biography 1949*. New York: H. W. Wilson, 1949, 473–475.

Three important histories of the search for the structure of DNA discuss Pauling's role in that event and his life and work in general. They are as follows:

Gribbin, John. *In Search of the Double Helix*. Aldershot, England: Wildwood House, 1985.

Judson, Horace Freeland. *The Eighth Day of Creation*. New York: Simon & Schuster, 1979.

Olby, Robert. *The Path to the Double Helix.* Seattle: University of Washington Press, 1974.

Some insight into Pauling's own thoughts is available in interviews that he has given with reporters for the popular media. These include:

Campbell, Neil A. "Crossing the Boundaries of Science." *Bio Science*, December 1986, 737–739.

Fry, William F., Jr. "What's New with You, Linus Pauling?" *The Humanist*, November/December 1974, 16–19.

Grosser, Morton. "Linus Pauling: Molecular Artist." *Saturday Evening Post*, Fall 1971, 147–149.

Hamilton, Mildred. "The Unretiring Paulings." *San Francisco Examiner & Chronicle*, August 21, 1977, 2 Scene.

Hogan, John. "Profile: Linus C. Pauling." *Scientific American*, March 1993, 36+.

"Interview: Linus Pauling." *Omni*, December 1986, 102–110.

"The Plowboy Interview: Dr. Linus Pauling." *Mother Earth News*, January/February 1978, 17–22.

Pogash, Carol. "The Great Gadfly." *Science Digest*, June 1981, 88–91+.

Ridgway, David. "Interview with Linus Pauling." *Journal of Chemical Education*, August 1976, 471–476.

Additional articles that provide further information about Pauling's personal and professional career include the following:

Allison, Helen C. "Outspoken Scientist." *Bulletin of the Atomic Scientists*, December 1960, 382+.

Beadle, George W. "Portrait of a Scientist—A Tribute to Linus Pauling." *Enginnering and Science*, April 1955, 11–14.

Goertzel, Ted G., Mildred George Goertzel, and Victor Goertzel. "Linus Pauling: The Scientist as Crusader." *Antioch Review*, Summer 1980, 371–382. See also the response to this article by Pauling in the Spring 1981 issue of this journal and Arthur Robinson's reply to Pauling in the Summer 1981 issue of the same journal.

Goodstein, Judith R. "Atoms, Molecules, and Linus Pauling." *Social Research*, Autumn 1984, 691–708.

Pauling has had, of course, an enormous impact on the institutions and fields of science with which he has been involved. The following reviews describe this impact for specific situations:

Gray, George W. "Pauling and Beadle." *Scientific American*, May 1949, 16–21.

Kalven, Harry, Jr. "Congressional Testing of Linus Pauling." *The Bulletin of the Atomic Scientists*, December 1960, 383–390.

Servos, John W. *Physical Chemistry from Ostwald to Pauling: The Making of a Science in America*. Princeton, NJ: Princeton University Press, 1990.

———."The Knowledge Corporation: A. A. Noyes and Chemistry and Cal-Tech, 1915–1930." *Ambix*, November 1976, 175–186.

INDEX

Illustrations are indicated by *italic* numbers.
The letter *g* after a number indicates a word in the glossary.